JUDICIAL
DICTATORSHIP

JUDICIAL
DICTATORSHIP

WILLIAM J. QUIRK
R. RANDALL BRIDWELL

TRANSACTION PUBLISHERS
NEW BRUNSWICK (U.S.A.) AND LONDON (U.K.)

First paperback printing 1997

Copyright © 1995 by Transaction Publishers, New Brunswick, New Jersey 08903.

This book is printed on acid-free paper that meets the American National Standard for Permanence of Paper for Printed Library Materials.

Library of Congress Catalog Number: 95-821
ISBN: 1-56000-225-5 (cloth); 1-56000-926-8 (paper)
Printed in the United States of America

Library of Congress Cataloging-in-Publication Data

Quirk, William J., 1933–
    Judicial dictatorship / William J. Quirk, R. Randall Bridwell.
        p. cm.
    Includes bibliographical references and index.
    ISBN 1-56000-225-5 (acid-free paper)
    1. United States. Supreme Court. 2. Judicial review—United States. 3. Political questions and judicial power—United States. 4. United States—Constitutional law—Interpretation and construction. I. Bridwell, R. Randall. II. Title.
KF8748.Q57 1995
347.73'12—dc20   95-821
                                                                        CIP

To my daughter, Augusta—WJQ

To my wife, Susan, my daughter, Sarah Margaret,
and my son, Philip—RRB

Acknowledgements

We would like to again thank John Montgomery, Dean of the School of Law, University of South Carolina, who encouraged us at every stage of this undertaking. We are indebted to the following students and former students who gave valuable help with the research on this book: Mike Polk, James Patrick, Carmen Tevis, and Shawn Dryer.

Several good friends followed the numerous drafts very closely, sacrificing many hours of their valuable time and making indispensable suggestions: John Eichner, Robbie Wilcox, Rick Handel, Ron Matthias, and Doug Parsons. Other friends read part of the manuscript and offered helpful suggestions: Tom Cherubini, Neal Hurwitz, Arthur Sporn, Tracy Herrick, Morris Handel, Matt Bruccoli, and Jim Berry. Thanks also to the staff of the New York Society Library on East 79th Street in New York City. Special thanks again to Arthur and Holly Magill for advice and friendship over the years. Additionally, the authors wish to especially thank Professor and Mrs. Thomas M. Lowry, Jr. for many years of wise counsel and good friendship.

Finally, we wish to thank the staff at the Law School for their dedicated efforts in the preparation of the manuscript, particularly Jimmie Sneed, Nancy Shealy, Frances Donnelly, and DeAnna Sugrue.

William J. Quirk
R. Randall Bridwell
September, 1994

Contents

Prologue

"If men were angels," James Madison wrote, "no government would be necessary." Or, "if angels were to govern men, no controls on government would be necessary." Madison assumed that men are about as good as they are going to be and, since no angels are available to rule, we need checks and balances.

Thomas Jefferson added the idea that sometimes "it is said that man cannot be trusted with the government of himself. Can he, then, be trusted with the government of others? Or have we found angels in the forms of kings to govern him." The Supreme Court claims the ultimate say in the American legal system through the doctrine of judicial review, which allows the Court to invalidate any state or federal law it considers inconsistent with the Constitution. Jefferson believed judicial review to be a very dangerous assumption of power by the Court which "would place us under the despotism of an oligarchy." To Jefferson, rule by a Supreme Court is no better than rule by an English king. Maybe worse, since nobody suggests the Court rules by divine guidance.

The purpose of judicial review is to restrain the will of the majority as expressed through the legislature and executive. Judicial review, as the phrase is used in this book, means the Court's power to rule federal and state laws and actions valid or invalid. The Court, of course, is supposed to review and interpret laws just as Congress is supposed to make laws and the executive is supposed to execute them. But the doctrine of judicial review gives the Court something the other branches do not have—the power to be the final authority of what the Constitution means. The other two branches, according to the theory of judicial review, are supposed to obey the Supreme Court. The theory derives its legitimacy from the argument that there must be a final arbiter of constitutional interpretation. Supporters of judicial review believe one branch, as a practical matter, has to have the last word and that the judiciary is the most suitable one. Finality, they say, is necessary to the system.

Jefferson, however, did not see it that way. He said that the sovereignty of the country, after the Revolution, passed from the king to the people. The people, by the Constitution, delegated power to three separate and independent branches. No branch is given power to control the actions of the others. The holder of a delegated power, Jefferson said, before he can act, must determine if the action is within the scope of his power. Each branch, therefore, has an equal power and obligation to interpret the Constitution on matters that come before it. The president and Congress are granted power by the people and are responsible to them. When he took office, Jefferson released everyone then imprisoned under the Alien and Sedition Laws—which the federal judiciary had held constitutional—because he said the laws were a "nullity, as absolute and as palpable as if Congress had ordered us to fall down and worship a golden image: and that it was as much my duty to arrest its execution in every stage, as it would have been to have rescued from the fiery furnace those who should have been cast into it for refusing to worship the image."

Judicial review assumes that the president and Congress, the branches responsible to the people, either cannot understand or will not respect the Constitution and the Supreme Court does understand it and will respect it. Judicial review today is almost universally accepted as part of the unwritten constitution created by John Marshall in *Marbury v. Madison* (1803). But maybe it's a disaster and we should forget it.

The philosophical assumptions of judicial review are so inconsistent with democratic theory that there is a long tradition of resistance to it. The resistance, today, is a largely underground movement that exists outside the normal academic and law school curriculum. Historically, the members of the resistance are an impressive group. They include the great democratic presidents: Thomas Jefferson, James Madison, Andrew Jackson, Abraham Lincoln, Theodore Roosevelt, and Franklin D. Roosevelt. They include the great constitutional scholars: James Bradley Thayer, "*The*

Origin and Scope of the American Doctrine of Constitutional Law" (1893) and *John Marshall* (1920); Louis Boudin, Government By *Judiciary* (1932); Edward S. Corwin, *Court Over Constitution* (1938); Henry Steele Commager, *Majority Rule and Minority Rights* (1943); and Learned Hand, *The Bill of Rights* (1958). Who made the Court, as Learned Hand asks: "the arbiters of all political authority in the nation with a discretion to act or not, as they please?"

For many years, judicial review, while fundamentally inconsistent with majority rule, was able to coexist with it, because of judicial self-restraint. For the past thirty years, however, the Supreme Court has used judicial review without restraint to impose basic social and economic policies on an unwilling majority. The Court, not the people, is now the agent of change in American society. The Court's policies, however, after thirty years, have not been successful.

What explains the country's long acquiescence in such an antidemocratic doctrine as judicial review? Or, more to the immediate point, is continued acquiescence a good idea? Would we be better off with a return to majority rule? The Supreme Court, as Professor Edward S. Corwin writes, has made itself "morally answerable for the safety and welfare of the nation to an extent utterly without precedent in judicial annals." The Court, as Professor Robert Nagel writes, "has isolated itself from the common man and the general culture, retaining ties of language and intellectual approach only to an academic elite." Three points are apparent.

First, our current system is not majoritarian, for it imposes unpopular policies upon the people. The current system is running counter to what Jefferson calls the "mother principle, that 'governments are republican only in proportion as they embody the will of the people, and execute it.'"

Second, the government, intellectuals (conservative and liberal) and the media support the Court's departures from majoritarian rule by disparaging the majority's ability to rule itself. These commentators agree with the Michael Kinsley view that the people want everything from government but don't want to pay. The people, they say, are no bargain. George Will, in *Restoration* (1992), writes that the "public mind is addled"; voters describe themselves as Jeffersonians favoring low taxes, no debt, and limited government, but on money measures, the "voters prove themselves ravenous for government" benefits. Jeff Greenfield writes, "No politician (and very few journalists) will ever acknowledge this, but one of the big problems with our form of government is that too many really, really stupid people get to vote." Alexander Hamilton, in a similar vein, wrote of the "amazing violence and turbulence of the democratic spirit." From Hamilton to Kinsley, the elite's central belief is that the people are such poor clay that it is ridiculous to try to follow Jefferson's "mother principle." The elite doesn't want a government that embodies the will of the people. They think it would be ugly.

Third, the opponents of majority rule believe that majority rule will harm the rights of the minority. They suspect that the majority is bent on depriving the minority of its rights and that only the nine Supreme Court justices prevent them from doing it. The elite's constitutional theory is accordingly simple—Thomas Jefferson wrote the Bill of Rights to enable the Supreme Court to protect the minority from the majority. Moreover, since protecting a minority is obviously preferable to oppressing one—and the Court's primary mission is the restraint of the majority—then it follows that the more times the Court decides against the majority the better.

This book expresses more confidence in the wisdom of majority rule. It challenges the assumption that, to avoid disarray, the Court must serve as a single final arbiter of the Constitution. Jefferson did write the Bill of Rights to protect the individual and restrain the federal government, but he did not think the Supreme Court had the exclusive authority to interpret it. The Constitution does not assign to any branch the authority to interpret its meaning. Jefferson wrote that each branch is "independent of the others and has an equal right to decide for itself what is the meaning of the Constitution in the cases submitted to its action." No branch has the absolute or final power to control the others, especially an unelected judiciary.

Jefferson, in 1823, wrote to William Johnson, explaining the critical conflict that existed even after the Revolution was successful:

The fact is, that at the formation of our government, many had formed their political opinions on European writings and practices, believing the experience of old countries, and especially of England, abusive as it was, to be a safer guide than mere theory. The doctrines of Europe were, that men in numerous associations cannot be restrained within the limits of order and justice, but by forces physical and moral, wielded over them by authorities independent of their will.   Hence their organization of kings, hereditary nobles, and priests.   Still further to constrain the brute force of the people, they deem it necessary to keep them down by hard labor, poverty and ignorance, and to take from them, as from bees, so much of their earnings, as that unremitting labor shall be necessary to obtain a sufficient surplus barely to sustain a scanty and miserable life.

"We believed," Jefferson continued, on the other hand, "that man was a rational animal, endowed by nature with rights, and with an innate sense of justice; and that he could be restrained from wrong and protected in right, by moderate powers, confided to persons of his own choice, and held to their duties by dependence on his own will." The Revolution, Jefferson said, was about self-rule.

Democratic government, Sidney Hook writes, is "not necessarily good government"; it is "sometimes foolish, sometimes callous and hostile to the underprivileged." A democracy may disintegrate from within because it makes unsuccessful choices, or makes excessive demands on government, or because of conflicting goals. Nonetheless, it is the faith of the democrat that self-government provides the "best, although far from perfect, way of getting good government." The fundamental challenge to democratic faith is from Plato and his philosophic descendants who "contend that most human beings are either too stupid or too vicious or both to be entrusted with the powers of self-government, and that ultimately the best interests of the people can be furthered by government of the learned, the wise and the virtuous." This hardy political perennial, Hook concludes, "blooms in many different forms of argument, and is found in both conservative and liberal color." Usually, the proponents of this view are whoever lost the last election.

The judiciary, led by the Supreme Court, is in the vanguard of the elite imposing nonmajority values and policies on the country. They are, as Jefferson said, the "miners and sappers" of democracy. The traditional view was that the separation of powers made the legislature and executive responsible for change and the Court the guardian of continuity and stability. The Court, however, over the past thirty years, has made itself the major agent for change—one that operates without democratic check to accomplish ends that could not be achieved by democratic process. Is the new system better than majority rule? Have we finally found angels in the forms of justices to rule us? This book tells that story.

1

Thomas Jefferson's Opinion of Judicial Review

> *Cherish therefore the spirit of our people, and keep alive their attention. Do not be too severe upon their errors, but reclaim them by enlightening them. If once they become inattentive to the public affairs, you and I, and Congress, and Assemblies, judges and governors shall all become wolves.*

—Thomas Jefferson to Edward Carrington
January 16, 1787

Jefferson and the Founders insisted on a written constitution because they believed it was the only safe way to institutionalize majority rule and to protect the people's liberties. The English constitution was unwritten, and the Americans thought they suffered greatly under it. Their overriding fear was of a despotic central government—like the Crown and the Crown's judges. They thought the written constitution, by clearly allocating power and rights, would prevent that.

The idea of a written constitution is a good one. England today works well without one, but it has had many centuries to develop, several revolutions, and one King's head cut off to help it come to an understanding of general principles. America has undoubtedly gotten a lot further faster because we started with a written constitution. It was certainly more efficient, and probably, in view of the experience under the Articles of Confederation, an absolute necessity, to start with an agreed statement of general principles.

But a written constitution works the way the Founders wanted only if there is no judicial review. If there is judicial review the situation reverses and the people are worse off than they would be with an unwritten constitution. Supreme Court justices, where there is no charter, have to justify their actions to a higher authority. If their government is a democracy—such as modern-day England—they must base each ruling on the statutes of Parliament. If the nation is not a democracy—such as feudal England—the judge still must act on behalf of ruling authority—the reigning king or queen. In either case, the judge's power could be corrected or reversed by the higher authority. Of course it is possible to have a constitution where the judges themselves rule without being subject to any higher authority. This would be a form of absolutism, like an absolute monarchy with more than one ruler, or like the ancient Judges of Israel. In America, under judicial review, the Supreme Court contends that the country's foundation document authorizes it to be the final interpreter of the meaning of that document. The Court says it is acting on behalf of a higher authority, the constitution, but, as a practical matter, it is not subject to correction or reversal.

When, judges assume a role as the final interpreters of the country's foundation document, they inextricably intertwine themselves with the document they interpret. The Court's opinions routinely employ the fiction that, when the justices speak, it is really the Constitution speaking through them. The practical effect is that to challenge the Court, one must appear to challenge the fundamental document itself. The natural reluctance to challenge the Constitution discourages a political response to the Court's rulings; these rulings are then enforced, whether persuasive or not.

Judicial review presents a critical "Who is to decide?" issue. The Constitution itself does not say who is to interpret it. It creates three separate and equal branches. It does not authorize one branch to bind the other two by its construction. John Marshall thought the Founders intended to give the Court the power to interpret the Constitution for the other branches but had inadvertently failed to write it in. Jefferson thought the Constitution's silence was exactly what was intended—that each branch had equal and unlimited authority to interpret the Constitution for its own purposes but that no one branch was set over the other two.

Jefferson, as a lawyer, understood that the power to construe or interpret a document is the critical power. The Constitution "is a mere thing of wax in the hands of the judiciary, which they may twist and shape into any form they please." The words will mean what the interpreter wants them to mean. The Constitution, if the Court has the ultimate say, is a Judicial Constitution. Jefferson wrote to Wilson Cary Nicholas on September 7, 1803, "Our peculiar security is in possession of a written Constitution. Let us not make it a blank paper by construction." Jefferson was familiar with the work of Bishop Hoadly, the seventeenth-century ecclesiastic, who wrote, "Whoever hath an absolute authority to interpret any written or spoken laws, it is He who is truly the Law-Giver to all intents and purposes, and not the person who first wrote or spoke them." Jefferson wrote to Judge John Tyler in 1810 that the law, in the hands of John Marshall, "is nothing more than an ambiguous text, to be explained by his sophistry into any meaning which may subserve his personal malice." Judicial review, Jefferson wrote, allows for a Supreme Court, "which from the citadel of the law can turn its guns on those they were meant to defend." Led by Marshall, the justices, by 1810, had "erected themselves into a political body with the assumed functions of correcting what they deem the errors of the nation."

A Judicial Constitution, of course, takes on a life apart from the words and a life apart from the people. Jefferson wrote to William Jarvis in 1820:

> It is a very dangerous doctrine to consider the judges as the ultimate arbiters of all constitutional questions. It is one which would place us under the despotism of an oligarchy.

Justice Joseph Story told Chief Justice Marshall that Jefferson's letter to Jarvis was publicly displayed in a bookstore and described it as shocking. Jefferson's purpose, said Story, was "to prostrate the judicial authority and annihilate all public reverence of its dignity."

Judicial review is incompatible with what we know the Founders did intend—federalism, majority rule, the sovereignty of the individual, the separation of powers and checks and balances. They did intend that each equal branch would check the other—that each had an independent power to determine the meaning of the

Constitution. Jefferson believed the Constitution intended concurrent review by each branch rather than judicial review; as he wrote in his First Annual Message to Congress, December 1801: "Our country has thought proper to distribute the power of government among three equal and independent authorities constituting each a check upon one or both of the others in all attempts to impair its constitution." He continued: "To make each an effectual check it must have a right in cases which arise within the line of its proper function where equally with the others it acts in the last resort and without appeal, to decide on the validity of an act according to its own judgment and uncontrolled by the opinions of any other departments." Jefferson, of course, recognized that conflict may well arise; that, however, will produce "less mischief than if one is set over the other." Surely, if the Founders had intended to set one branch over the other they would have said so. Surely, as a matter of democratic theory, Jefferson is right that the elected branches can not be less equal than the judiciary. The elected branches must have rights at least equal with unelected judges to determine the meaning of the constitution. Judicial supremacy, said Jefferson with inexorable logic, could not, over the long run, coexist with democracy.

In a letter to Spencer Roane, Jefferson, then age seventy-five, sharpened the point: it is "an axiom of eternal truth in politics, that whatever power in any government is independent [unchecked], is *absolute* also: in theory only, at first, while the spirit of the people is up, but in practice, as fast as that relaxes" (emphasis added). Judges who could not be removed, are "the most suspect source of decision in a democratic government." Judges are "effectually independent of the nation." Finally, the "most suspect source of decision" remains suspect even if it is made up of the best men in the country: "it is the office of a good judge to enlarge his jurisdiction."

The trouble with judicial review is the same thing that was wrong with the rule of the American colonies by the British Crown, over whom Americans had no control, and rule by Parliament, within which they had no representation. As far as Americans were concerned, the British constitution was completely nondemocratic. At heart, of course, the Jefferson-Republicans opposed judicial review for the same reason they opposed the English Crown—it prevented self-government. Madison wrote to William Eustis from Montpelier on May 22, 1823:

> There has been a deep distinction between the two parties [Republican and Federalist]. . . . The distinction has its origin in the confidence of the former [Republicans] in the capacity of mankind for self-government, and in a distrust of it by the others or by its leaders; and is the key to many of the phenomena presented by our Political History.

Jefferson's and Madison's basic theory of divided and checked power makes no sense if judicial review is right. The whole point of their constitutional theory is to prevent absolute—or unchecked—power in government. Jefferson wrote to Spencer Roane, the independent power can be "trusted nowhere but with the people in mass."

The Supreme Court's power to say what the Constitution means is called here absolute, or unchecked, because it is beyond the national majority's control. Article V of the Constitution requires a two-thirds vote of both houses of Congress to propose an amendment to the Constitution, and ratification by three-fourths of the states. The Equal Rights Amendment, despite majority support, failed to be adopted after two tries. Similarly, the Balanced Budget Amendment is still struggling. Both of these amendments would be part of our Constitution if a simple referendum majority were sufficient. The final problem for those who follow the amendment route is that after adoption, the same Court that caused the original grievance is authorized by judicial review to interpret the meaning of the new amendment designed to correct it. This may explain why we have had so few amendments. The process is daunting and the prize at the end of the road may be illusory. "The salient characteristic of the United States constitution," according to the 1911 *Encyclopedia Britannica*, is "its formidable apparatus of provisions against change."

Absolute power is wrong in itself, regardless of whether its holders are well intentioned. Guardians can be smarter than most of the people—and better intentioned—but rule by guardians is not a system for a free people. Jefferson wrote to the Marquis de Lafayette that "the good sense of our people will direct the boat ultimately to its proper point." Jefferson understood that a democratic people will, at times, make errors, but as he wrote to

Edward Carrington on January 16, 1787: "Do not be too severe upon their errors, but reclaim them by enlightening them. If once they become inattentive to the public affairs, you and I, and Congress, and Assemblies, judges and governors shall all become wolves."

Judicial review, in the hands of a "strict constructionist" judge, is like a loaded gun: dangerous, but not necessarily fatal. The modern Supreme Court justices, however, speak of a "living" constitution. By this, they mean they are free to apply current standards—theirs—to fill in gaps in the Constitution, or even to overrule parts of it.

In recent years, some justices of the Supreme Court have been surprisingly open in their opposition to democracy. Justice William Brennan, on October 12, 1985 told a Georgetown Law School audience he believed capital punishment is "under all circumstances cruel and unusual punishment prohibited by the Eighth Amendment." This conclusion ignores the Fifth Amendment express provision of the that people will have to answer for capital crimes with appropriate safeguards: "No person shall be held to answer for a capital, or otherwise infamous crime, unless on a presentment or indictment of a Grand Jury . . . nor be deprived of life, liberty or property, without due process of law." Justice Brennan, on the other hand, believes that capital punishment is "an absolute denial of the executed person's humanity" and "irreversibly degrading to the very essence of human dignity":

> A punishment must not be so severe as to be utterly and irreversibly degrading to the very essence of human dignity. Death for any crime whatsoever, and under all circumstances, is a truly awesome punishment. The calculated killing of a human being by the state involves, by its very nature, an absolute denial of the executed person's humanity. The most vile murder does not, in my view, release the state from constitutional restraints on the destruction of human dignity. Yet an executed person has lost the very right to have rights, now or ever.

So has the victim.

Justice Brennan further noted that the "majoritarian process has appeal under some circumstances, but I think ultimately it will not do." He explained: "Faith in democracy is one thing, blind faith quite another":

The majoritarian process cannot be expected to rectify claims of minority right that arise as a response to the outcomes of that very majoritarian process.

The majority, Justice Brennan believes, is bent on denying rights to the minority. Justice Brennan told the Georgetown Law School audience what he saw as the inequities of majority rule:

Unabashed enshrinement of majority rule would permit the imposition of a social caste system or wholesale confiscation of property so long as a majority of the authorized legislative body, fairly elected, approved. Our Constitution could not abide such a situation. It is the very purpose of the Constitution and particularly the Bill of Rights—to declare certain values transcendent, beyond the reach of temporary political majorities.

We current justices read the Constitution the only way we can: as twentieth-century Americans. We look to the history of the time of framing and to the intervening history of interpretation. But the ultimate question must be, What do the words mean in our time?

For the genius of the Constitution rests not in any static meaning it might have had in a world that is dead and gone but in the adaptability of its great principles to cope with current problems and current needs. Our Constitution was not intended to preserve a preexisting society but to make a new one.

The Court's role, as explained by Justice Brennan, to declare "certain values transcendent" and "beyond the reach of temporary political majorities" is not consistent with Jeffersonian democracy. It gives the Court a tremendous amount of power. Would an angel really want that kind of power?

The position of the modern justices is, at best, less than candid. For while expressly claiming wide—indeed overriding—discretion, their only claim to authority is the 1787 document. But that document was written by a world that Justice Brennan tells us "is dead and gone." The modern justices believe they should apply current standards to the old document. They are a strange group of runaway agents claiming authority their principal never gave them under a document which they feel free to rewrite and reinterpret without any check or balance.

John Marshall, in *Marbury v. Madison* (1803) said the Constitution is the "fundamental and paramount law of the nation," and it is "emphatically the province and duty of the judicial department to say what the law is." The Court added, in *Cooper v. Aaron*, (1958), that the "federal judiciary is supreme in the exposition of the law of the Constitution" and this is a "permanent and indispensable feature of our constitutional system." The Court noted that government officials are "solemnly committed by oath" to support the Constitution. Justice William O. Douglas wrote in *We, the Judges* (1956): "The Judiciary is in a high sense the guardians of the conscience of the people as well as the law of the land." If the Court keeps the conscience of the people, who keeps the conscience of the Court?

The Court, however, believes, as Yale Professor Alexander Bickel wrote in his book, *The Least Dangerous Branch*, that it is "empowered to lay down the law of the land, and citizens must accept it uncritically. Whatever the Court lays down is right, even if wrong, because the Court and only the Court speaks in the name of the Constitution." The Court's decision necessarily cuts off public debate and the possibility of achieving a democratic consensus. Professor Bickel writes: "The Court has spoken. The Court must be obeyed. There must be good order and peaceable submission to lawful authority." It is a very volatile mix when the power of coercion is tied to a Court which believes, with Justice Brennan, that its obligation is to find "certain values transcendent" and place them "beyond the reach of temporary political majorities." And if the people, who are told they must uncritically accept the Court's decisions, in fact believe the Court has separated itself from the concerns of the common man and is no longer acting in his best interest, then we are in the middle of a constitutional crisis.

The crisis is very well defined. Madison said a republic was a "government which derived all of its powers directly or indirectly from the great body of the people." Jefferson, as noted earlier, said that "governments are republican in proportion as they embody the will of their people and execute it." Justice Brennan thinks such blind faith in democracy is misplaced. The will of the people is likely to be oppressive. He believes the Court was established to protect the victims of majority oppression. The argument that the removal of the judicial check would leave our government an unlimited one is, as Professor Commager wrote in *Majority Rule and Minority Rights* (1943), "almost deliberately malicious." A large part of American politics is "concerned with reconciling majority and minority will, class hostilities, sectional differences, the divergent interests of producer and consumer, of agriculture and labor, of creditor and debtor, of city and county, of taxpayer and tax beneficiary, of the military and civilian"; in short, the natural checks and balances of democratic politics.

As already noted, judicial review is greatly assisted by the public reluctance to tinker with a Constitution that is viewed with great respect. However the document is interpreted, there is a willingness to accept the interpretation given rather than challenge the infallibility of the document. That attitude toward the Constitution however has not always existed. Jefferson believed that a constitution derives "its obligation from the will of the existing majority" which led to his idea of remaking the constitution every generation. Jefferson thought we would need a revolution or a change of constitution every generation. The constitution was not, he said, the "arc of the covenant, too sacred to be touched." Jefferson envisioned a constitution that would keep pace with the times, but do so through the will of the people rather than a ruling oligarchy. This fit his philosophy that the "earth belongs to the living." One generation he wrote, is "as capable as another of taking care of itself, and of ordering its own affairs." He wrote to Madison in 1789 that "no society can make a perpetual constitution, or even a perpetual law. The earth belongs always to the living generation." For this reason, Jefferson believed that the constitution would need changing every generation. Jefferson, when he wrote that governments derive "their just powers from the consent of the governed" meant actual consent. The people's actual and continuing consent was necessary to the legitimacy of the government.

Jefferson's idea of remaking the constitution every generation, of course, deprives judicial review of its practical usefulness, that is, that some of the change it brings fits the current generation better than the 1787 Constitution. The strength of Jefferson's idea is that change will come from the consent of the governed rather than judicial rule.

When the Court declares a "right," for example, that an atheist has a right to a city hall park free of créches or a criminal has a right that evidence of a crime be excluded from his trial because it was wrongfully obtained, the Court's rule is backed by the government's coercive power. The Court's rule binds all. A person's demand for freedom of speech, as Sidney Hook writes, "is at the same time a demand that the freedom of those who desire to prevent [him] from speaking should be curbed." What is a "right"? Jenny Teichmann, in the December 1993 *New Criterion*, writes: "Ordinary people go around claiming all sorts of rights that nobody ever heard of before: the right to be respected, the right to vacations, to fun, etc." Talking about rights is "a way of saying what you think ought to be done." What "ought to be done," of course, sounds like a legislative, not judicial, function. For the past thirty years, however, the judiciary has granted many more "rights" than the legislature.

The Court, as the holder of ultimate power, retains full discretion to decide any case in any way or not to decide a case. It may make up a new test; it may find one side or the other has failed to meet some "balancing" test, but next time perhaps they can add a little weight and prevail. But then again, perhaps not. Jefferson thought the role of judges is to "render the law more and more certain" not to wander around "with pretorian discretion." A court which exercised such discretion, he wrote to Philip Mazzei, November 28, 1785, "would be a monster whose existence should not be suffered one moment in a free country wherein every power is dangerous which is not bound up by general laws."

Jefferson believed the president had an equal right with the other branches to determine the constitutionality of legislative acts. He would not enforce a law that he believed was unconstitutional. Upon his election, he released every person in jail, or being prosecuted, under the Alien and Sedition Laws. He wrote to Abigail Adams, July 22, 1804, as noted above, that law was a "nullity, as absolute and as palpable as if Congress had ordered us to fall down and worship a golden image: and that it was as much my duty to arrest its execution in every stage, as it would have been to have rescued from the fiery furnace those who should have been cast into it for refusing to worship the image." He elaborated in his First Annual Message to Congress:

> On my accession to the administration, reclamations against the sedition act were laid before me by individual citizens claiming the protection of the Constitution against the sedition act. Called upon by the position in which the nation had placed me to exercise in their behalf my free and independent judgment, I took that act into consideration, compared it with the

Constitution, viewed it under every respect of which I thought it susceptible, and gave it all the attention which the magnitude of the case demanded. On mature deliberation, in the presence of the nation and under the solemn oath which binds me to them, and to my duty, I do declare that I hold that act to be in palpable and unqualified contradiction to the Constitution.

Nothing in the Constitution, Jefferson wrote to Abigail Adams, gave the judges power "to decide for the Executive, more than to the Executive to decide for them." The executive is accountable to the people. They will decide if he has gone beyond the power granted to him.

If the judiciary is independent and must interpret the Constitution for its own purposes, are not the other two branches equally independent? If the judiciary can examine the acts of the legislature and executive why can't those branches examine the acts of the judiciary? If the elected branches violate the Constitution, as Jefferson said he did in making the Louisiana Purchase, they must "risk themselves like faithful servants . . . and throw themselves on their country for doing for them unauthorized, what we know they would have done for themselves had they been in a situation to do it." The people, if they did not agree, could not give the Louisiana territory back to Napoleon, but they could punish the president who bought it.

Jefferson wrote to Edward Carrington on January 16, 1787:

I am persuaded myself that the good sense of the people will always be found to be the best army. They may be led astray for a moment, but will soon correct themselves. The people are the only censors of their governors: and even their errors will tend to keep these to the true principles of their institutions. To punish these errors too severely would be to suppress the only safeguard of the public liberty.

The people "may be led astray for a moment but will soon correct themselves." In a democracy, as far as Jefferson was concerned, the people would correct themselves, but their governors would not. In 1781, Jefferson wrote in *Notes on Virginia*:

In every government on earth is some trace of human weakness, some germ of corruption and degeneracy, which cunning will discover, and wickedness insensibly open, cultivate, and improve. Every government degenerates when

trusted to the rulers of the people alone. The people themselves therefore
are its only safe depositories. And to render even them safe their minds must
be improved to a certain degree.

The judiciary, however, is immune from popular correction.
Our judges are given lifetime tenure and can be impeached only for
misconduct. Indeed, today, a federal circuit judge who serves fifteen
years is guaranteed a pension at full judicial salary, $140,000. As
Jefferson wrote to Samuel Kercheval in 1816, we have made judges
"independent of the nation itself." Judicial independence of the will
of the nation, he wrote William T. Barry, "is a solecism in a republic
of the first order of absurdity and inconsistency." Jefferson's letter
to Kercheval explained that in England, lifetime tenure for judges
was a useful reform while in the United States it "operates in an
opposite direction":

> In England, where judges were named and removable at the will of an
> hereditary executive, from which branch most misrule was feared, and has
> flowed, it was a great point gained, by fixing them for life, to make them
> independent of that executive. But in a government founded on the public
> will, this principle operates in an opposite direction, and against that will.

Jefferson, in an 1819 letter to Spencer Roane, denied the judiciary
"the right they usurp of exclusively explaining the constitution." If
judicial review is correct, "then indeed is our constitution a complete
felo de se [Suicide or, literally, one who commits a felony against
himself]":

> For, intending to establish three departments, co-ordinate and independent,
> that they might check and balance one another, it has given, according to this
> opinion, to one of them alone, the right to prescribe rules for the government
> of the others, and to that one too, which is unelected by, and independent of
> the nation.

Each branch receives its power from the people delegated by
them through the constitution. The holder of a delegated power, of
course, must decide before he acts, whether or not the proposed
action is within his grant. He may be wrong, but if he is, he's
accountable to the grantor and no one else. The branches are
separate and coequal and the grantor is the people; the executive
and legislature are directly accountable to the grantor.

The Supreme Court could not order Congress, Jefferson wrote, "to pass laws for a census, for paying the judges and other officers of government, for establishing a militia, for naturalization as prescribed by the constitution, or if they fail to meet in Congress, the judges cannot issue their mandamus to them." Nor can the Court order the president if he "fails to supply the place of a judge, to appoint other civil or military officers [or] to issue requisite commissions." All the departments, Jefferson wrote, are "co-equal and co-sovereign within themselves."

Jefferson, in his 1801 draft of a message to Congress, explained his concurrent review theory:

> Our country has thought proper to distribute the powers of its government among three equal & independent authorities, constituting each a check on one or both of the others, in all attempts to impair its constitution. To make each an effectual check, it must have a right in cases which arise within the line of its proper functions, where, equally with the others, it acts in the last resort & without appeal, to decide on the validity of an act according to its own judgment, & uncontrolled by the opinion of any other department. We have accordingly, in more than one instance, seen the opinions of different departments in opposition to each other, & no ill ensue. The constitution, moreover, as a further security for itself, against violation even by a concurrence of all the departments, has provided for its own reintegration by a change in the persons exercising the functions of those departments.

Dumas Malone, in *Jefferson the President* (1970), writes that Jefferson deleted the passage quoted above from the final message to Congress because he believed the opposition would consider the language an "avowal of arbitrary presidential authority." Jefferson further explained what Malone calls his tripartite theory in the 1804 letter to Abigail Adams:

> The judges, believing the law constitutional, had a right to pass a sentence of fine and imprisonment, because that power was placed in their hands by the constitution. But the Executive, believing the law to be unconstitutional, was bound to remit the execution of it; because that power has been confided to him by the constitution. That instrument meant that its co-ordinate branches should be checks on each other. But the opinion which gives to the judges the right to decide what laws are constitutional, and what not, not only for themselves in their own sphere of action, but for the legislature and executive also in their spheres, would make the judiciary a despotic branch.

Malone notes that Jefferson's theory of constitutional interpretation may seem vague and remote to modern jurists. But in his day, and for some decades thereafter, "it approximated the actualities of the governmental situation." To "all practical purposes the legislature and the executive continued to determine for themselves whether or not they were acting within the bounds of the Constitution. Marshall's words of warning in the Marbury case may have caused them to be more careful, but the constitutional significance of these words really lay in the distant future."

Learned Hand largely agreed with Jefferson's analysis of judicial review. In *The Bill of Rights* (1958), Hand wrote that judicial review is not supported by the text of the Constitution, or the theory of democracy. It certainly does not accord, Hand continued, "with the underlying presuppositions of popular government to vest in a chamber, unaccountable to anyone but itself, the power to suppress social experiments which it does not approve." The Constitution does not authorize the Court to "assume the role of a third legislative chamber." But Hand thought judicial review a practical necessity in extraordinary cases. Each branch exercising its independent power to interpret the Constitution could lead us, in practice, to two or three different interpretations. Jefferson recognized that was possible when he declared the Alien and Sedition Laws unconstitutional while Congress and the federal courts thought they were valid. Certainly, the branches could come into sharp conflict. That was not neat and symmetrical, but was it so terrible? The theory of checks and balances, after all, assumes a good deal of bumping. Similarly, the theory of federalism assumes some conflict between the states and the federal government. It could be useful and lived with. Conflict, after all, is not just unpleasant, it is the way free people move toward a consensus. In any case, Jefferson wrote in a letter of June, 1815 to William Torrance that it would produce "less mischief than arises from giving to any one of them a control over the others":

> It may be said that contradictory decisions may arise in such case, and produce inconvenience. This is possible, and is a necessary failing in all human proceedings. Yet the prudence of the public functionaries, and authority of public opinion, will generally produce accommodation.

Jefferson's theory builds in a bias against change in the law. That is, under his approach, each branch has to decide for itself that the law is constitutional before the branch can act with respect to it. The legislature has to believe the bill is constitutional before it passes it; the court has to believe the law is constitutional before it orders compliance; and the executive has to believe it is constitutional before it enforces it. If any one of the branches concludes the law is unconstitutional the law does not become operative. Jefferson's approach favors limited government. Under judicial review, on the other hand, one branch (the Court by itself) or two branches at the most (the Court together with either the executive or legislature) are enough to start society marching off down a new road. The government will be more energetic.

There is a philosophical gulf between the two positions. The judicial review bias is preferred by those who think change should come from the top and are not that concerned about compelling people to do things they don't want to do. The Jeffersonian bias is preferred by those who believe change should come by private, and voluntary acts. Laws—which will be enforced against those who don't want them—should only be used where it is absolutely clear that a consensus exists.

Learned Hand's constitutional law teacher, Professor James Bradley Thayer, made the same point in his book *John Marshall* (1920):

> It should be remembered that the exercise of [the power of judicial review], even when unavoidable, is always attended with a serious evil, namely that the correction of legislative mistakes comes from the outside, and the people thus lose the political experience, and moral education and stimulus that comes from fighting the question out in the ordinary way, and correcting their own errors. The tendency of a common and easy resort to this great function . . . is to dwarf the political capacity of the people, and to deaden its sense of moral responsibility.

The Court, in forcing its decisions upon an unwilling majority, deadens the people's sense of moral responsibility and dwarfs its political capacity.

Hand, in a 1933 nationwide radio address, explained that the Founders intended a government that would "express the common will of the people who were to rule":

They wanted to have a *government by the people*, and they believed that the only way they could do it, was by giving the power to make laws to assemblies which the people chose, directly or at second hand. They believed that such assemblies *would express the common will of the people who were to rule.* Never mind what they thought that common will was; *it is not so simple as it seems to learn just what they did mean by it,* or what anybody can mean. *It is enough that they did not mean by it what any one individual, whether or not he was a judge, should think right and proper.* They might have made the judge the mouthpiece of the common will, finding it out by his contacts with people generally; *but he would then have been ruler, like the Judges of Israel.* (Emphasis added)

Government is the mechanism through which the community employs force. It uses force against its foreign enemies and against its own people. The government provides a means of coercion, and coercion naturally leads to resistance. Jefferson and the Founders thought the king and his judges had unjustly used force against them—to take their property, to take their lives. The Founders' solution, after getting rid of the king, was to establish that all laws had to have the consent of the governed. They did not want to bring back the Judges of Israel. The citizen could not be shoved around unless a majority of his fellow citizens thought it was in furtherance of a necessary rule. Law, Marsilius of Padua wrote in 1324, will be "better observed by every citizen which each one seems to have imposed upon himself." John Wildman, in the 1647 Debates held by Cromwell's Army at Putney, asked: "Whether any person can justly be bound by law, who doth not give his consent that such persons shall make laws for him?"

The Founders also tried to assure limited government—limited in the things it was supposed to undertake—delegated powers—and in the means it could use to achieve them—federalism, separation of powers, and checks and balances. The courts, on the other hand, use force freely and without consent. The courtroom is not a place where ideas are exchanged and debated in a free atmosphere. The dominant emotion around a courthouse is one of stark fear. The dominant atmosphere is one of submission to the authority of the presiding judge. The courtroom is a poor place for deciding society's basic social and economic policies. For that reason, it was not the one chosen by the Framers to serve this purpose.

The Founders intended that it be very hard to get a law passed. For that reason they divided the mistrusted legislative power into two chambers. That also was to assure full consideration and the development of a consensus in support of it. But it is very easy to get an order from a district court judge in a constitutional case, just the filing of a few pieces of paper. The judiciary is designed to settle private disputes between private parties. The parties do not represent anyone but themselves, and a judge's order deciding an issue between them should not have any impact on anyone else. The judge does not consider the cost, or who, outside the courtroom, will be hurt by it. The court's decision is final. A law, however, may be altered or repealed as soon as the losing side can gather enough votes. The lack of finality is a critical part of the democracy. There is always the hope for the losers that tomorrow may be better, and the recognition by the winners that their power may be fleeting.

Democracy, as Jefferson and Madison conceived it, is a political system that mediates the differences in society. Over the past thirty years, however, the political system has been largely replaced by the legal system. The Court has successfully competed with the political system by granting remedies previously available only through the political process. The legal system, however, does not mediate differences, it creates winners and losers. For example, suppose some convicts think they are over-crowded. To secure more space from the political system, they would have to persuade a majority that it was fair, and the majority would have to agree to issue bonds or raise taxes. The convicts, to secure majority support, might well have to compromise their claims. If the convicts seek a judicial solution, however, the court can give them a complete remedy despite the fact they lack popular support. The Court makes a new judicial plan and orders the majority, whose own plan is at the same time overturned, to pay for it. The Court may be right, in some abstract or real sense, but its decision does not rest on a democratic consensus. The Court aggravates, rather than mediates, differences. As the judiciary controls more and more areas, the society becomes more and more divided. In the process, the Court collapses the political system. Our basic reliance on a system for throwing our representatives out does not work if the ones we can throw out do not have the real power.

Jefferson wrote to Archibald Thweat on January 19, 1821:

The legislative and executive branches may sometimes err, but elections and dependence will bring them to rights. The judiciary branch is the instrument which, working like gravity, without intermission, is to press us at last into one consolidated mass.

Jefferson said "energetic" government is always oppressive. The democratic consensus on most issues at most times favors inaction. Inaction indicates the majority's belief either that the good to come of intervention is not clear enough or the cost, financial or in terms of freedom, is too great. The courts, however, when a complaint is filed, have to give an answer. The court's agenda is set by the individual, governmental agency, or private group bringing the complaint.

The Founders hated the king's judges at least as much as the king. They designed the legislature to make laws. The members are supposed to represent the people of their districts. The introduction of a bill gives the public notice that its interests may be altered. A proposed law may arouse fears among those who will be hurt by it. Marsilius of Padua wrote: "anyone can look to see whether a proposed law leans towards the benefit of one or a few persons more than of the others or of the community, and can protest against it." Congress is set up to hear from its constituents, hold hearings, and consider what the law will cost and whom it will hurt. The Founders' purpose was to assure that any law—which of necessity was going to be enforced against those who didn't want it—would be fully considered and supported by a consensus of public opinion. It is supposed to be very hard. Normally the process requires a good deal of compromise. If a majority is not satisfied with the results, it can always refuse to return the representative who voted for it, something it can never do with a federal judge.

The judiciary, since it operates by diktat, does not need to develop a consensus to support its rulings. Indeed, judicial intervention will short-circuit a developing political consensus. For example, in the early 1970s, New York and a dozen other states had developed majorities to agree on some form of legal abortion. The issue was very difficult but the democracy was working it out. The Supreme Court, however, in its 1973 *Roe v. Wade* decision removed abortion from the political process by finding it to be constitutionally regulated. Following that decision, the winners didn't need the political process, and it couldn't help the losers. Because it is not based on consent, *Roe v. Wade* has festered for twenty years of bitterness and violence. Those, such as Justice Brennan, who criticize a majoritarian legislative process for not rectifying "claims of minority right" certainly cannot argue that a decision by a majority of judges operates any more effectively in that regard.

Beginning in the 1960s the Court rather than the legislature became the main mechanism for change. In a recent *U.S. News & World Report* article, John Leo writes, "reformers now routinely skip the legislative process and take their issues directly to Court." The reformers believe that since "majorities are wrongheaded and oppressive . . . why not try for a judge imposed quick fix?" The Court-imposed solutions, however, writes Mr. Leo, "lack the stability of a social consensus, they often just breed more trouble"; they run into severe resistance.

The independent judiciary holds power without commensurate responsibility—an awkward combination in a democracy. Because the Court does not need public consent, because a decision only requires five votes, and because its orders are imposed by force, the Court will do things a legislature would never dream of. The Court's foray into judicial governance, not surprisingly, has been singularly unsuccessful as well as undemocratic.

The justices also reserve the discretion to act or not, as they please. For example, the Court avoided ruling on the constitution-ality of the undeclared war in Vietnam. When it chooses not to rule, the Court simply denies the petition for a hearing or says the plaintiff lacks "standing" or that the issue is a "political question." These doctrines sound like there is something to them, but they are inventions of the Court and are controlled by it—they bind the Court as long as it wants to be bound. The Court can avoid hard cases and those that would require it to define its position. The power to refuse to rule allows the Court to keep a lot of distance between itself and the people—it needn't even answer their questions.

In a Jeffersonian world, relations between people are based on consent and agreed upon norms. In a judicial world that is not necessarily so. For example, an agreed upon norm is that state discrimination on the basis of race is immoral, unconstitutional and wrong—the great majority of Americans believe the state must be colorblind. The Court's 1954 decision in *Brown v. Board of Education* had majority support in all regions of the country outside the South. Indeed, the Court's slowness in overruling its 1896 decision in *Plessy v. Ferguson*, (Louisiana law requiring railway companies to provide "separate but equal" accommodation for the "white and colored races" found consistent with the Fourteenth Amendment), and its original mistake in deciding that case, show it to have an imperfect moral compass. The Court combines bad attributes from several systems—it acts much too slowly in cases of clear wrong, yet when it does act, the change comes abruptly because the judicial process does not develop any democratic consensus in the country as it goes along.

Events of the mid-twentieth century illustrate both the enormous powers usurped by the Court in its currently assumed role and the broad gulf that can exist between accepted public norms and judicially imposed policies. The Civil Rights Act of 1964 provides that any activity receiving federal funds must also be colorblind:

> No person in the United States shall, on the ground of race, color, or national origin, be excluded from participation in, be denied the benefits of, or be subjected to discrimination under any program or activity receiving Federal financial assistance.

The act further noted that nothing in its text shall be interpreted "to require any employer . . . to grant preferential treatment to any individual or to any group on account of an imbalance which may exist with respect to the total number or percentage of persons of any race, color, religion, sex or national origin."

The statute accurately captured the basic American faith in equality before the law and equality of opportunity. The heart of Jefferson's democratic faith and revolutionary promise is the liberation of the human spirit from oppression, from any chains that hold the individual back from where his merit and hard work will take him. In America, the individual was going to have sufficient freedom to develop his talents and abilities. Jefferson intended to build a nation on one idea—the dignity of the individual. As Lincoln told the Ohio troops: "I am living witness that any one of your children may look to come here as my father's child has. . . . that each of you may have, through this free government . . . an open field and a fair chance for your industry, enterprise, and intelligence." Andrew Jackson, when he vetoed the Bank Bill in 1832, wrote: "Distinctions in society will always exist under every just government. Equality of talents, of education, or of wealth can not be produced by human institutions. In the full enjoyment of the gifts of Heaven and the fruits of superior industry, economy, and virtue, every man is equally entitled to protection by law; but when the laws undertake to add to these natural and just advantages artificial distinctions . . . to make the rich richer and the potent more powerful, the humble members of society—the farmers, mechanics, and laborers—who have neither the time nor the means of securing like favors to themselves, have a right to complain of the injustice of their Government." Eric Hoffer, in 1968, said, "you just cannot conceive what this country has meant to the common man."

In 1965 Lyndon Johnson turned the ship of state from the old course, Lincoln and Jackson's equality of opportunity, to a different port, equality in result. The liberal objective shifted from nondiscrimination to entitlements. Johnson, on June 4, 1965, told a Howard University audience that the Voting Rights Act of 1965 would be

not the end . . . not even the beginning of the end. But it is perhaps the end of the beginning. . . . That beginning is freedom; and the barriers to that freedom are tumbling down. . . . We seek not just legal equality but human equality, not just equality as a right and a theory but equality as *a fact and equality as a result*. (Emphasis added)

The people never agreed to that. Every poll ever taken shows that 80 percent of the people do not agree with that. Nothing in the Constitution said that. None of the statutes that Congress had passed said anything like that.

Johnson, as the executive, chose a political course that challenged the democratic consensus. Johnson's challenge was not as straightforward as Jefferson's rejection of the Alien and Sedition Laws but the people understood it. They could support Johnson's new approach or stick with Jefferson and Lincoln and Jackson. The American people repudiated Johnson at the first opportunity. In

1964, he received 43,000,000 votes (61 percent) against Goldwater's 27,000,000 (39 percent). In 1968, of the 43,000,000 who had voted for him in 1964, 28 percent, or 12,000,000, deserted his party. In the 1968 election, Nixon received 32,000,000 (43.4 percent); Humphrey—31,000,000 (42.7 percent) and Wallace 10,000,000 (14 percent). The 1968 election, Theodore H. White wrote in *The Making of the Presidency*—1968, was a first in America history—a "negative landslide." Added together, the Nixon-Wallace vote came to 56.9 percent against Humphrey's 42.7 percent. What did the vote mean? The Vietnam War was the critical issue to the public but the parties did not offer any clear choice—Nixon, cryptically, said he had a plan he could not disclose and Humphrey was very unclear as to what differences he had, if any, with Johnson's policy. The parties did differ, and the election turned on, racial issues, law and order, and civil peace. The only two repudiations comparable to Johnson's were Herbert Hoover's, 1928-32, which involved a depression, and Woodrow Wilson's, 1916-20, which involved a world war.

The system, however, worked only until the Supreme Court intervened to impose its will upon the people. Unwilling to leave office in shame, as Johnson had, the Court instead undertook to impose Johnson's failed policy on the country—to shift the basic idea of America from individual inalienable rights to group rights supervised by the Court. In 1970, without any explanation, the Court moved from *Brown's* principle which outlawed discrimination based on race to a new rule mandating a racially determined result. Nondiscrimination, or colorblindness, is a unifying principle since it doesn't ask anything special for one group as opposed to another. It just asks for equal treatment. Racial entitlement is a divisive principle since it makes special claims based on group membership, some are entitled and the rest are not. The Court, in its 1970 decision in *Swann v. Charlotte-Mecklenburg Board of Education* classified students by race and authorized busing to accomplish racial balance. The Court intervened although it was well aware of the developing rift between itself and the people. Every poll ever taken reports that about 80 percent of all parents prefer neighborhood schools to busing. The Court's orders were nonetheless enforced.

Beginning in 1970, the Medical School of the University of California at Davis set up a racial plan that specifically reserved sixteen of its one-hundred slots for minorities. Allan Bakke, a white male, applied to Davis in 1973 and 1974 and was denied admission although his test numbers were just below the average of regular admittees and well above the average of the special admittees. Bakke argued that the California quota plan violated the Equal Protection Clause of the Fourteenth Amendment and the antidiscrimination provisions of the 1964 Civil Rights Act.   The Supreme Court in its 1978 decision, *California Regents v. Bakke*, endorsed racial plans for government and publicly supported universities. Justice Brennan wrote: "Government may take race into account when it acts not to demean or insult any racial group but to remedy disadvantages cast on minorities by racial prejudice." Justice Blackmun added the sentiment: "In order to get beyond racism, we must first take account of race. There is no other way. And in order to treat some persons equally, we must treat them differently. We cannot—we dare not—let the Equal Protection Clause perpetuate racial supremacy." Thus, the Court achieved what President Johnson had been unable to achieve.   It drafted into American law the principle that equality of opportunity is inadequate. In essence, the Court concluded that we can't have a fair race—all starting from the same starting line—because, due to past disadvantages, some of the runners are slower.

A year later, in *United Steelworkers v. Weber*, the Court pushed racial plans into the private workplace.   In 1974 the United Steelworkers and Kaiser Aluminum included an affirmative action plan in their agreement establishing how production workers could enter into craft training. The plan reserved for black employees 50 percent of the openings in in-plant craft-training programs until the percentage of black craft workers in a plant equaled the percentage of blacks in the local labor force. Brian Weber said that junior black production employees were receiving craft training in preference to senior white employees. He said the Civil Rights Act of 1964 made it unlawful to "discriminate . . . because of . . . race."   The lower courts agreed with Weber, holding that all employment preferences based upon race violated the statute's prohibition against racial discrimination.   The Supreme Court reversed.   Justice Brennan conceded—he didn't have much choice—that Weber's argument, relying on a "literal construction" of the statute, was "not without force." But Justice Brennan said that what Weber didn't understand was the "spirit" of the statute:

> It would be ironic indeed if a law triggered by a Nation's concern over centuries of racial injustice and intended to improve the lot of those who had "been excluded from the American dream for so long," 110 Cong. Rec. 6552 (1964) (remarks of Sen. Humphrey), constituted the first legislative prohibition of all voluntary, private, race-conscious efforts to abolish traditional patterns of racial segregation and hierarchy.

Jefferson said the function of the judge is to make the law more and more certain. Justice Brennan believes the function of law is "to declare certain values transcendent [and] beyond the reach of temporary political majorities." Brennan's ruling gives vast power to the executive department (the Equal Employment Opportunity Commission) to impose racial plans on private employers. The only way the employer can avoid legal expense is to hire by the numbers. Every large and medium-sized corporation in the country has adopted some form of quota system. The American Society of Newspaper Editors, the *New York Times* reported in April 1994, has implemented a program to assure 30 percent minority employees in the country's newsrooms by the year 2000. The country's opportunity system, in both public and private employment, has changed from a system based on Jeffersonian merit to one based on an assortment of preferential treatment, quotas, entitlements, and protected classes. How can a society make progress if the individual is not entitled to equal citizenship—equal representation—and equal economic opportunity? How can it say it is treating its citizens fairly?

Jefferson, as noted earlier, said Judicial Review was a "very dangerous doctrine . . . which would place us under the despotism of a oligarchy." The oligarchy's current high spirits are described in Nat Hentoff's 1991 *Playboy* interview with Justice Brennan. Hentoff writes he has "never known anyone who loved his work" more than Brennan. A couple of years ago, as they were walking out of the Supreme Court building, Brennan took Hentoff by the elbow, looked around the marble hall, and said, "this is just incredible being here—I mean the opportunity to be a participant in decisions that have such an enormous impact on our society." Was a kid at F.A.O. Schwarz ever so happy?

Why didn't the people respond by asking Congress to reverse *Bakke* and *Weber*? While the opinions were far from clear, the Supreme Court did not find that minorities had a constitutional right to affirmative action and quotas. Congress, as a technical matter, at least, could have repassed the 1964 Civil Rights Act language and said we really mean it this time. But the question was, could a new law help? If the Fourteenth Amendment means anything it means the state cannot deny a citizen "the equal protection of the laws" based on race. The Court, however, had just held that discrimination, if it was well motivated, was acceptable. The Court's equal protection theory opened up such a philosophical chasm between itself and the rest of the country that no reasonable person could believe that a new statute or a new Amendment would make any difference. The Court had made clear it intended to implement a policy of racial balancing.

President George Bush, for twenty months, called the bill that became the Civil Rights Act of 1991 a "quota" bill for private employers. The bill, after a small change of language in October 1991, was passed with bipartisan support. President Bush said the small change turned a bad quota bill into a good civil rights bill but, to most observers, it was still a quota bill. This suggests that Congress, if it understood what was going on, now buys into *Bakke*-style race consciousness.

Congress is at least ambivalent on racial plans. The 1982 amendments to the Voting Rights Act of 1965 provide that the "extent to which members of a protected class have been elected" in state or city elections may be considered in determining whether the "protected class" has "less opportunity" to elect representatives of its choice. That language, while hardly lucid, seems to authorize the Justice Department to impose "proportional representation"—if the "protected class" has not been successful in past elections. For example, South Carolina's legislature must contain the same 30 percent black membership as the general population does. But Congress, contradictorily, added that the above-quoted language does not establish a right to have members of a "protected class" elected in numbers equal to their proportion of the population. In *Shaw v. Reno* (1993) the Supreme Court added to the confusion by avoiding the main issue—whether racial gerrymandering is a violation of the

Fourteenth Amendment—and ruling the district court should redraw North Carolina's serpentine I-85 congressional district because it was "tortured," "irrational," and "bizarre"—a standard geared to aesthetics that could swing with the viewer. The result of the confusing statute and decision is that proportional representation is either constitutionally mandated or a constitutional violation.

In 1990, the Court, in *Metro Broadcasting v. FCC*, upheld FCC regulations, based on statute, granting preferences to minority-owned business in applying for radio and television broadcasting licenses. The Court found that increasing minority ownership would help diversify broadcast program content. The use of racial distinctions, to increase diversity, the Court concluded, is not a constitutional evil. Justice Stevens wrote, "neither the favored nor the disfavored class is stigmatized in any way." The disfavored class, however, might consider the lack of a license to be financially stigmatizing. In 1993 Congress ordered the FCC to set up a system of preferences for small business, minorities and women for the auctions of 2,000 licenses for wireless telephone and data communications.

The polling, however, continues to report that 80 percent of the public do not support racial plans. Perhaps Congress has a more accurate reading of the public, in which case, even if the Court loses its power as ultimate arbiter, the country would keep all the racial plans, protected classes, preferences, and quotas it now has. On the other hand, the polling may accurately reflect the majority will and if the Court's special power is removed, it would mean an end to quotas in the United States.

There may be good arguments to make for racial plans and quotas, but the majority didn't buy them in 1978 or now. The Court's decisions polarized the issue and cut off an on-going public debate. The winning side had no reason to compromise with the losers, since the winners had the state's coercive power behind them. The losers, the unprotected and unpreferred, had nothing to bargain with. The Court's intervention prevented the possible development of a democratic consensus behind some kind of racial plan.

The Supreme Court, under judicial review, is able to do *more* than change the rules we live under—how we elect local governing bodies, state legislators, or congressmen, how and where our children are educated, who pays for it, and so on. The judiciary has also taken control over the most fundamental principles we live under. Do we have common citizenship of equal legal and political rights for individuals protected by a Constitution, or do we have a confederation of competing groups whose legal status and political rights are managed from above? In short, do we have a government based on the "consent of the governed," a democracy, as Jefferson said? Or do we have "angels in the form of men sent to govern us?" Democracy, as Jefferson wrote, involves more than procedure. Jefferson designed the procedure to fit his conception of the nature of man. A democracy will support one system of values, and a nondemocratic system quite another.

Basic change, in a legislative and democratic world, has to be debated. The opinions of judges should be influential to the extent they are persuasive. But, as Herbert Croly wrote in *Progressive Democracy* in 1914, "The words of judges, which are uttered in the name of the people, but without their express understanding, can have no permanently and sufficiently formative effect of public opinion."

Croly wrote, "A social program becomes dangerous to popular liberty [if] it is not authorized by the free choice of the popular will." Democracy, Croly notes, "does not consist of a devouring popular sovereignty to which all limitations are essentially obnoxious. Many severe limitations are imposed upon it as a condition of its own self-expression. But democracy as a living political system does demand the effective recognition of ultimate popular political responsibility." A government based on force, not consent, Jefferson wrote to Madison on January 30, 1787, "is a government of wolves over sheep."

2

The Rule of Five: The Rise of
Federal Judicial Power

*All our political experiments rest on the capacity
of mankind for self-government.*

—James Madison, *The Federalist*, No. 39

*I have no fear that the result of our experiment
will be that men may be trusted to govern
themselves without a master. Could the contrary
of this be proved, I should conclude either that
there is no god, or that he is a malevolent being.*

—Thomas Jefferson, letter to David Hartley,
July 2, 1787

Judges, in Europe, do not declare legislative acts to be illegal. In England, Parliament exercises the ultimate sovereignty of the country. A European intellectual, looking at our Court's unreviewable power to do so, would probably say America is an operating judicial dictatorship. The legislature in the U.S., he would say, can raise taxes and build roads but the important questions, those that decide what kind of country it is, all end up in the Supreme Court. We would answer that the Court is the "least dangerous" branch as Alexander Hamilton said; it has no executive or legislative authority; it doesn't make rules; it just decides cases that come before it. The trouble with our answer is that the Court is able to select the cases that come before it from a large number of them. The Court, at its 1992-93 term, refused to hear 7,233 cases while it decided to hear ninety-seven, or 1.3 percent. In 1950, on the other hand, the Court heard 10 percent of the cases brought to it which indicates it was then acting as a court of appeal over the lower federal courts. The Court's power to pick from among such a large number of cases gives it the practical ability to rule on issues it thinks important, to act, in effect, as a Court of National Policy. The Court, of course, may have the power to pursue a legislative agenda, but not exercise it. On the other hand, the Court may be deciding a lot of things the legislature should be deciding.

Judicial review, as Hamilton explained it in *The Federalist* No. 78, was not intended to block the majority or protect the minority. It was to prevent the legislature from overstepping the authority the people had given them. The judiciary, he wrote, "from the nature of its function, will always be the least dangerous to the political rights of the constitution." The executive holds the sword of the community and the legislature the purse: "The judiciary, on the contrary, has no influence over either the sword or the purse; no direction either of the strength or of the wealth of the society; and can take no active resolution whatever." The courts, he said, "may truly be said to have neither FORCE nor WILL but merely judgment; and must ultimately depend upon the aid of the executive arm for the efficacious exercise even of this facility." The judiciary is therefore the "weakest of the three branches."

But where does the Court get the power to determine the meaning of the Constitution for the other two branches? Hamilton did not cite anything in the text; he began, however, with an unarguable proposition—that every act of delegated authority contrary to the principal's instruction is void, and that, therefore, no legislative act, contrary to the constitution, can be valid. Otherwise, as Hamilton said, the deputy is greater than his principal, the servant above his master and the "representatives of the people are superior to the people themselves." It would violate this principle to say that the "legislative body are themselves the constitutional judges of their own powers, and that the construction they put upon them is conclusive upon the other departments."

So far, so good. Jefferson agreed with the argument to this point. But not with the next step. Hamilton went on to explain his theory that the Court is entitled to decide for the other two branches: "the courts were designed to be an intermediate body between the people and the legislature, in order, among other things, to keep the latter within the limits assigned to their authority." The "interpretation of the laws is the proper and peculiar province of the courts", and a "constitution is in fact, and must be regarded by the judges as a fundamental law." This does not, Hamilton concluded, make the judicial superior to the legislative—it "only supposes that the power of the people is superior to both." The Court is enforcing the Constitution *on behalf of* "the people," according to Hamilton, but the problem is that Hamilton's "people" is an abstraction, they don't actually exist. It is the nine justices, or five of them, who say what the people mean. As Justice Brennan told his law clerks: "With five votes around here you can do anything."

Hamilton assumes the Court will not make itself "superior to the people themselves." But if such a power threatens the authority of the people when held by a legislature, who must stand for election, why is the same power no threat to democracy when held by an unelected Court? Jefferson believed there is no "least dangerous branch"; each branch is dangerous if removed from the checks of democracy expressed by the other two branches and the people themselves.

Jefferson did not believe that judges were angels; "[O]ur judges are as honest as other men, and not more so. They have, with others, the same passions for party, for power, and the privilege of their corps. Their maxim is 'boni judicis est ampliare jurisdictionem [a good judge will enlarge his jurisdiction].'"

Why has Hamilton's argument prevailed? Hamilton's point about the settling effect of one branch having the final word is appealing, almost like the practical necessity of parents running a household. But the situations are not similar—families don't claim to be democracies. Hamilton's argument, indeed, in view of the Court's current dominant power, seems disingenuous, or, as Chief Justice Hughes said, "almost ironic." Justice Brennan does not sound like an "intermediate body" when he talks about declaring "certain values transcendent" and beyond the "reach of temporary political majorities."

Exactly what is the Court supposed to protect us from? "I have scant fear," said Theodore Roosevelt, "of the tyranny of the majority."

Sidney Hook writes that the "dictatorship of the majority" haunts "the books of political theorists but has never been found in the flesh in modern history." While a majority in a democracy is free to oppress a minority, it will very seldom want to do so. As issues change, so does the majority; every vote, of necessity, creates a minority. Some mainstream issues—such as safety in the streets, the education of children, the basic security of the society—are supported by almost everyone and don't normally have an oppressive potential. Beyond that, on most other issues, there is no one majority. Any individual who is in the majority on one vote understands that he may be in the minority on the next issue. The Bill of Rights was demanded by several states as a condition to approval of the Constitution because the majority wanted to protect the rights of the minority. The citizen knew he was going to often be in the minority.

The cost of oppression will normally exceed any benefits realized from the exercise of such power. A minority in a democracy has the power to impose costs upon an oppressive majority, and to make its resistance felt if it feels oppressed. The costs of running a police state are very high. If a group believes the majority is consistently unfair to it, it has five basic options. It can: (1) accept what the majority has relegated it to; (2) try to change the majority's mind; (3) resort to civil disobedience; (4) leave; or (5) revolt. Another option, if the minority is able, is to steal the next election. Historically, this is a popular and successful option.

Civil disobedience, revolt, emigration impose a real cost upon the majority, and the likelihood of such a response will be weighed by the majority in deciding whether to impose oppressive rules. The majority will modify its treatment of any person or group if it is persuaded that its treatment is unfair, unwise, or immoral. In our current system, however, even where the minority has failed to persuade the majority to alter its conduct, the Supreme Court may intervene and grant the minority what the majority won't provide. The criminal, for example, is granted freedom; the pornographer, the right to publish; the prisoner, a comfortable cell. The Court, in essence, substitutes its judgment of right and wrong for that of the majority.

The ultimate question in a democracy is how much power the current majority has. A constitution distributes political power and describes the basic procedures to be followed in its exercise. Also, the Constitution sets out certain individual freedoms that are supposed to be beyond the power of the majority to interfere with, the Bill of Rights. Finally, we were taught, the Supreme Court is to delineate those individual freedoms protected by the Constitution and protect them from the will of the majority. This system, in theory, is supposed to leave the individual a lot of freedom to deal with life's problems.

Every reader probably will agree with those principles as a general matter. Yet every reader will also agree, if he thinks about it, that, in fact, the majority today has only the most tentative kind of power. It has, for example, no final power over criminal justice, education, taxation, voting, employment, immigration, and deportation. The majority can take initial action, but it is up to the Supreme Court to make the final decision. They may find a "constitutional right" and find that the majority's plan violates it. End of majority's plan.

The Court is usually described in political terms—"conservative," "liberal," "moderate," "activist," "restrained"—but the political labels cover up the real problem, which is that the Court may be whatever it chooses—it has the unlimited power to define its own powers. *Nil Ultra*—Nothing higher. The issue is the Court's power rather than its orientation. Power may be limited in a constitution, but orientation cannot. Neither can orientation be predicted when power is not limited. The Court's power is so great that it might corrupt an angel.

The Senate, appropriately, deals with nominees to the Court as political appointments. The senators want to know if the justice will vote for the policies they agree with. The Republican party, since 1968, has gained many presidential votes on its promise to appoint "restrained" or "original intent" justices. The theory went that the new appointees, if they could get a majority, would rein in the out-of-control court—children would go to neighborhood schools and criminals would go to jail. The Republicans appointed every justice between 1968 and 1992—ten new angels. The results, however, are less than heavenly—the little children are still bused and criminals still walk if the constable stumbles. The trouble, as Sidney Hook points out *The Paradoxes of Freedom* (1962), is that "the *theory* of judicial restraint is unsatisfactory." The doctrine is unable to "formulate a clear and valid criterion" to describe when the Court will intervene. Its deference to Congress is laudable but it is a "self-imposed deference with very elastic limits."

Appointing "strict construction" judges is a feckless solution by the majority to the problem of a Court that consistently supports the minority view on education, crime, and cultural issues. "Strict construction" is the natural cry of a minority, not a majority. In the past, when the Court overruled the majority—for example, in *Lochner* and the substantive due process cases—Theodore Roosevelt's suggested solution was to change the structure to make it more responsive by giving the people the power to overrule the Court (to be discussed below at 50-53). A democratic solution to an out-of-control court is not to change the membership of the body that is abusing its power. A democratic solution would reduce its power or make it accountable. As John C. Calhoun pointed out, "strict construction" is a "phantom," a thing "good in the abstract, but in practice not worth a farthing." Everybody is for strict construction "but in fact, it will ever be found to be the construction of the permanent minority against the permanent majority, and of course of itself valueless."

The appointment route is also pointless because the so-called "conservative" justices are as antimajority as the so-called "liberals." For example, Justice Antonin Scalia, the leading intellectual of the "conservative" justices, on May 6, 1994 told the Commonwealth Club of San Francisco that an "evolving" or "living" Constitution "will always make a majority happy." That seems an exaggeration. But it is, he continued, "quite mad" and "will destroy us because the whole purpose of the Bill of Rights is to prevent the majority from doing what it thinks ought to be done." If a living Constitution makes the majority happy, why are they miserable? And if the Bill of Rights is intended to aggravate and frustrate the majority, why did the majority adopt it?

Some large differences between what the Founders intended and what we have now, are clear and no longer controversial. The Founders, as the reader was taught in sixth grade civics, had a great fear of power because of their experience with King George. They believed that power ultimately resides in the people. Government was delegated certain powers to be exercised as specified. First, they divided up power, and then hedged it, so the American state could not oppress the individual. They divided power between the states and the national government. They called this the federal system, and gave the national government a group of defined powers. These included the power to make war, treaties, currency, and to regulate commerce between the states and with foreign nations. All residual powers remained with the states. Second, they divided federal power into three parts, executive, legislative, and judicial. Together, these devices of separated powers with checks and balances, and limited taxing authority, were intended to check the national power. The Founders intended to brake the power of both the executive and the national legislature. Madison argued in *The Federalist* No. 51 that "usurpations are guarded against" by the distribution and division of power to the different branches on each level:

> Hence a double security arises to the rights of the people. The different governments will control each other; at the same time that each will be controlled by itself.

The intended limitations on the judiciary were less defined but clear. George Bancroft describes the views of the Constitutional Convention on judicial power in his 1885 *History of the United States* as follows:

> The judiciary passes upon every case that may be presented, and its decision on the case is definitive; but without further authority over the executive or the legislature, for the convention had wisely refused to make the judges a council to either of them.

The failure to expressly check the power of the judiciary, however, has allowed the Court to expand the power of the other federal branches, and in doing so, to expand its own powers.

In Jefferson's time, prior to the Fourteenth Amendment, the Constitution defined the powers of the federal government, but not the states. To Jefferson, the common law was the basic source of law, and it operated from the bottom up since it was simply the community's established customs and procedures. State common law flourished, but was kept in check by the ever-present threat of legislative reversal if the courts' interpretation of the common law strayed too far from fundamental principles held by the majority. The federal judiciary did intervene under extraordinary circumstances, for example, if a state imposed a tax on the national bank, the Court would uphold the national power. The national court, as Jefferson said, was on every occasion, driving the country into consolidation. But basically the federal courts had little everyday business to do. The country ran successfully with very little judicial interference with the majority will. The Court, after *Marbury* in 1803 did not declare another federal law unconstitutional until *Dred Scott* in 1857. After the Civil War, the Fourteenth Amendment opened the door to a new era of constitutionally based federal control over state actions. As the arbiter of the federal constitution, the significance of the federal courts rose and federal judges slowly assumed a much greater control over the country. The federal judges, because of judicial review, were not checked by the legislature, as the state courts had been.

The mechanism for everyday federal control over state and local majorities is the Fourteenth Amendment, adopted in 1868. The Bill of Rights Amendments only restrained the actions of Congress and the federal government. The Fourteenth Amendment, however, imposed federal power over the action of the states. It provides that no state shall "deprive any person of life, liberty or property without due process of law, nor deny to any person within its jurisdiction the equal protection of its laws." Those words are very general; what do they mean? Initially, in the 1873 *Slaughter-House Cases*, the Court said it did not find in that language "any purpose to destroy the main features of the general system" the Founders had established. The Louisiana legislature had granted one company a slaughter-house monopoly, thereby putting its competitors out of business. The competing butchers claimed Fourteenth Amendment protection against the legislative power of their own state which had deprived them of their livelihood. The Louisiana law was hardly appealing but the Court upheld it, saying that to hold otherwise would be "so great a departure from the structure and spirit of our institutions; when the effect is to fetter and degrade the State governments by subjecting them to the control of Congress" and would constitute "this court a perpetual censor upon all legislation of the States." In less than twenty years, however, as discussed below, the Court reversed itself and took up the "perpetual censor" role that it enjoys today.

The Fourteenth Amendment was also the wedge for bringing over the Bill of Rights restraints to apply them to state and local governments. The Bill of Rights, adopted in 1791, prohibited the federal government from interfering with specified inalienable rights, such as the freedoms of speech and religion. The Bill of Rights did not limit the power of the states. The state constitutions and courts, from 1791 to 1937, determined the extent to which a state would enjoy free speech and religion and the other Bill of Rights provisions. Theoretically, a state could have adopted a state religion or established procedures to suppress free speech. Or it could have taken its citizen's property without compensation. No state, of course, wanted to do those things; the people had no interest in self-imposed tyranny. Each state's constitution protected against those things. America, before the 1937 federal judicial takeover, was a constitutional democracy. The Fourteenth Amendment broke up the old system; it required the states to afford to their citizens "due process of law" and "equal protection of the laws," as found by the federal judiciary. The Supreme Court, in the 1937 decision of *Palko v. Connecticut*, began to "incorporate" the Bill of Rights provisions into the Fourteenth Amendment through the due process clause. This meant the Bill of Rights limits, after 1937, applied to state and local governments to the extent the federal judiciary determined. Incorporation added more vague words—freedom of religion, freedom of speech, right of assembly, unreasonable searches, double jeopardy, self-incrimination, and liberty and due process to the vague words of the Fourteenth Amendment—property, liberty, due process again, and equal protection. Beginning around 1890, the Court used these indefinite words to defeat majority positions. From 1890 to 1937, the Court used the Fourteenth Amendment to throw out state social and economic legislation such as child labor laws. It used the theory that freedom of contract was part of "liberty," and could not be taken without due process. The Court, under severe pressure from Franklin Roosevelt, deserted this line in 1937. However, almost immediately it developed a new and more intrusive theory—that while it agreed to restrain itself on economic regulation, it would not restrain itself with respect to what it called "personal" rights. The Court said these "personal" rights were more important than property rights. The "personal" rights found in the Bill of Rights, the Court said, had a preferred status. The Court, since *Palko,* extended the Bill of Rights to state and local government, was able to enforce such broad concepts as freedom of speech, as it interpreted them, against a state and local majority as well as against the national majority.

Learned Hand, writing in 1946, said just why "property itself was not a 'personal right' nobody took the time to explain." Hand believed the Bill of Rights "could not be treated like ordinary law, its directions were to be understood rather as admonitions to forbearance." Its terms were too sweeping and the power it would allocate to the Court too great. The extent of the Bill of Rights protections and their enforceability should be left to the legislature. The other side, Hand conceded, had some logic to it. After all, "the Bill of Rights was law, and not merely a counsel of perfection and an ideal of temperance: always to be kept in mind it is true, but whose infractions were to be treated only as a matter for regret." Hand responded that, however that might be, that view had to be rejected in order to preserve the whole system   The effect of adopting it would make "the courts a third camera—in fact final arbiters in disputes in which everybody agreed they should have no part." The courts, if they upset majority solutions "under cover of the majestic sententiousness of the Bill of Rights . . . are likely to become centers of frictions undreamed of by those who avail themselves of this facile opportunity to enforce their will." At least, after Hand's writing, the stakes were clear. The justices who routinely overturned the majority's solutions could not claim to be well intentioned but short sighted. After Hand, they knew their acts ran the risk of damaging the democracy.

Hand's Bill of Rights theory is one way to deal with a basic inconsistency in American political theory. It was perfectly reasonable for the barons at Runnymede to force King John to grant them a charter of rights which limited the King's sovereign powers. It would have been unreasonable for the barons, and they didn't consider it for a minute, to agree with each other to limit their own baronial power. But that is about what we did. In America the people, the source of power, voluntarily agreed to limit their power. Our two fundamental principles are: first, the government rests on the consent of the governed as expressed by majority rule in the Federal   and   State   Constitutional   Conventions   and   in   their ratification; second, there are certain inalienable rights which are exempt from governmental control and are defined in the Bill of Rights. If everything falls within the first principle there could be no room for inalienable rights. If everything falls under the second principle there could be no room for consent of the governed. Taken together, wrote Federal District Judge Charles E. Wyzanski, Jr. in the 1944 *Harvard Law Review*, "these principles necessarily imply that the majority of the persons living at any particular time have the right to determine the rules which shall prevail in society except upon certain matters, such as the right of free speech, which are beyond the proper scope of any government or any majority at any time." The critical issue, the one this book is about, is who determines whether particular action of government goes beyond its proper powers and regulates inalienable rights. Who decides the extent of the majority's self-imposed restraints? John Marshall's answer was that's the judiciary's job, which means the judges, as Jefferson said, are "effectually independent of the nation." Marshall's answer inexorably leads to judicial supremacy which, as Hand said, brings the judges into "disputes in which everybody agreed they should have no part." Hand's answer was to remove the conflict by considering the Bill of Rights as admonitions intended to guide all the branches of government, but not to be enforced. Jefferson's answer had two closely related parts. First, his basic tripartite theory, rejecting judicial review, meant that all three separate and equal branches would have to agree before the government could act. That meant conflict was reduced because governmental action was reduced. And second, his basic theory that the earth belongs to the living, and that each generation should shape its own law and constitution, meant that the definition of inalienable rights would stay close to the control of the majority. The consent of the governed is continuing and current, and the people can correct any mistakes the judges or their representatives make.

As a general matter, Jefferson believed that if there was doubt as to the existence of a constitutional power, it ought not to be exercised. He wrote to Edward Livingston in 1824 respecting the national power to make internal improvements such as roads and canals. Jefferson believed this power was basically benign but he noted that many opposed it and believed it to be based on an "elaborate construction" of the constitution. The wisest course was to ask the people for an express grant of the power: "A government held together by the bands of reason only, requires much compromise of opinion; that things even salutary should not be crammed down the throats of dissenting brethren."

The Founders clearly intended a limited national power, but it is equally clear we are operating with an unlimited one. There are no serious limits on the national power—that issue was decided against the Founders a long time ago. In 1941, the constitutional historian, Professor Edward S. Corwin wrote, in *Court Over Constitution*: "the National Government is entitled to employ any and all of its powers to forward any and all of the objectives of good government."

Because the Hamiltonian version of judicial review, rather than the Jeffersonian one, has prevailed, the judiciary, has the final word on its own power and that of the other branches of the federal government. The Court formed an unholy alliance with the other branches. As it expanded their power, it expanded its own. Rather than being checked by coequal branches of government, so that the final scope of national power is defined by the actions of all three branches, judicial review allows the Court to set the limits of governmental power. Yale Professor Charles L. Black, Jr. wrote in *The People and the Court* (1960):

> What a government of limited power needs, at the beginning and forever, is some means of satisfying the people that it has taken all the steps humanly possible to stay within its powers. That is the condition of its legitimacy, and its legitimacy, in the long run, is the condition of its life. And the Court, through its history, has acted as the legitimator of the government. In a very real sense, the Government of the United States is based on the opinions of the Supreme Court.

It seems almost safe to say that the opinions of the Supreme Court *are* the government of the United States.

The Court's power, and the national power, were originally held in place by a series of specific barriers as well as the principles of federalism and the separation of powers. The central government, during the nineteenth century, largely because of the Civil War, gained substantial powers, but the specific barriers that limited it were not directly challenged. They were challenged and began falling in the 1920s, by the late 1930s and early 1940s they were falling fast; and by the 1960s they were all gone. The old barriers were:

(1) *Defined Power*: The Founders were very clear that the national government was granted only defined powers and the states reserved all the powers not granted. This barrier collapsed when the Court's 1923 decision in *Massachusetts v. Mellon*, determining that the spending power was not limited to acting in aid of a specified defined power, but could be in aid of the "general welfare" clause. (2) *The Commerce Clause* : One of the defined powers given to Congress is the power "to regulate commerce" between the states.   How expansively could you read that?   In the 1942 case of *Wickard v. Filburn*, the Court held that a farmer growing wheat for his family had an effect on interstate commerce which authorized regulation of his planting. The Court also held that the commerce power can be used to regulate matters with slight or no apparent relation to commerce, for example, the transportation of plural wives across state lines by Mormons in *Cleveland v. U.S.* (1946) and banning racial discrimination in motels, local restaurants, and recreation parks on the ground that food served had ingredients from other states: *Heart of Atlanta Motel v. U.S.* (1964), *Katzenbach v. McClung* (1964), and *Daniel v. Paul* (1969) (Justice Black's dissent in *Daniel* said there was no finding that an interstate traveler had ever visited the park which lay in a sleepy hollow in the Arkansas hills, miles away from any interstate highway).

The Court was able to roll through the restraining barriers because it defines and creates its own powers. The theory of judicial review grants the Court the unreviewable power to interpret the words of the Constitution. It is able, as Jefferson warned, to "make [the Constitution] a blank paper by construction."

At first, the Court acted with the support of the majority. The majority wanted governmental action taken, in the 1930s, to ameliorate the Depression and, in the 1950s, to end discrimination. Perhaps there was enough popular support to push through needed constitutional amendments to authorize the action. Perhaps there was not. The Court, by interpretation, extended the national majority's power without amendment. The Court assumed the *de facto* power to amend the Constitution without securing ratification from three-fourths of the states. The problem with such a power is that it can be used as easily to subvert majority will as to support it.

The Court deleted the limits on the central power—federalism, the power of the states, and, at the national level, the separation of powers. The Court reversed the Founders' basic theory that governmental power should be spread around. Jefferson wrote in *Notes on Virginia*, that the "powers of government should be so divided and balanced among several bodies of magistracy, as that no one could transcend their legal limits, without being effectually checked and restrained by the others." The division of governmental power was critical to the Founders; Jefferson said an *"elective despotism* was not the government we fought for" (emphasis in original).

The 1789 French Constituent Assembly, on the other hand, created an unlimited national legislature. Article II of the Declaration of Rights read that the "principle of sovereignty resides essentially with the nation." Article VI added that "law is an expression of the general will." Under the French approach, Aleksandr Solzhenitsyn writes in *Rebuilding Russia* (1991), deputies were cut off from their voters and from any personal responsibilities toward them. They are "merely a part of that collective body which in fact is the will of the people." The American constitutional historian, B.F. Wright wrote in *Consensus and Continuity, 1776-1787* (1958) that the only limitation upon the expression of power by the French national legislature "seems to be the will of the nation which is to say, the law of the national legislative body. The only effective restriction, other than the power of the suffrage, would seem to be revolution."

The American Constitution established a government limited in its objects, its methods, and its taxing power. What the limited government limits is majority rule, that is, the majority agrees, in making a constitution, that it will not ask government to go beyond the stated objects and methods. The majority was out of line when it asked the Court to go beyond the original agreement. The majority got its way, but, by allowing the Court the power to usurp the amendment process, and condoning a Court that defined its own powers, the majority unleashed a force it could not control. The new creature, in a short time, turned on its master.

In its 1954 decision, *Brown v. Board of Education*, the Court held unconstitutional state laws requiring racial segregation. Gallup reports that a strong majority of the public supported *Brown* in all regions of the country outside the South. *Brown*, in retrospect, is the high watermark of majority power. From 1937 until, and including *Brown*, the national power generally supported majority interests. But after *Brown*, as the memory of Roosevelt's attack faded, the Court returned to the doctrine that it should be a bulwark against an oppressive and irresponsible majority.

The Court, certainly since the 1960s, has been in the vanguard of what Professor Paul Hollander, in his 1992 book *Anti-Americanism*, calls the "adversarial culture." The "adversarial culture" says Hollander is an intellectual elite that believes the "prevailing social order is deeply flawed, unjust, corrupt and irrational, calculated to constrain or reduce human satisfactions." The adversarial culture believes, Professor Hollander writes in *Society* magazine (1992), the "United States is a uniquely deformed, exceptionally irrational, corrupt and unjust society." The culture is driven by a "profound sense of alienation, a hostility toward dominant American institutions and values as they existed before the 1960s." The elite believes it is better than the common man because it is brighter and more compassionate. Theodore H. White, writing in *The Making of the Presidency, 1968*, expressed the same thought: "Out of cynicism and despair, the new avant-garde has come to despise its own country and its traditions as has rarely happened in any community in the world; American institutions, customs and laws are regarded as the greatest system of restraints on that individual self-expression which it sees as the highest right of man." The Court's role, as part of the adversarial culture, is to be the guardian of the conscience of the country. Under judicial review, the social views of the "adversarial culture" work their way into constitutional law. In March 1994, the Court unanimously overturned a lower court's judgment that the rap group 2 Live Crew had infringed the copyright of Roy Orbison's 1964 song "Oh, Pretty Woman." The rap group version, the Court found, could fall under the fair use doctrine that allows part of a copyrighted work to be used without permission for purposes of criticism, comment, news-reporting, teaching, scholarship, or research. The 2 Live Crew version changed the original's pretty woman walking down the street into a "big hairy woman," "bald- headed woman," and "two-timing woman." In *Campbell v. Acuff-Rose*, Justice Souter said: "The later words can be taken as a comment on the naiveté of the original of an earlier day, as a rejection of its sentiment that ignores the ugliness of street life and the debasement that it signifies." The Court's words can be taken as a comment on how far a group of judges can remove themselves from the way ordinary people think.

The Court styles itself as the protector of individual rights and self-expression against the will of the oppressive bourgeois majority. Crime, in this context, is a form of self-expression as well as social protest and criticism. The Court routinely overrules the actions of the local police, boards of education, and the state laws under which they act. The beneficiaries of the Court's protection are criminals, atheists, homosexuals, flag burners, Indians, illegal entrants, including terrorists, convicts, the mentally ill, and pornographers. The Court calls the deleted state laws "arbitrary," or "without rational basis," extravagant language which, as Professor Robert Nagel points out in his 1989 book, *Constitutional Cultures*, shows no respect for the acts of popular assemblies. The Court's attitude is the opposite of Learned Hand, who believed "that a law which can get itself enacted is almost sure to have behind it a support which is not wholly unreasonable." The Court, as Professor Nagel notes, has acted "to isolate itself from the general culture, retaining ties of language and intellectual approach only to an academic elite."

The Court often finds as facts things that very few people in the country believe are facts. For example, in May 1994, a federal district court ordered the Washington National Guard to reinstate a lesbian nurse because the military's policy against homosexuals was based solely on prejudice. The court found that "there is no rational basis for the Government's underlying contention that homosexual orientation equals 'desire or propensity to engage' in homosexual conduct." Most people, however, judging from their own propensi-ties, are fairly certain that orientation does equal desire.

The majority has given the Court's policies a fair chance to work—thirty years. The Court's policies, however, have not been successful. The Court's failure is disturbing since the primary areas the Justices took over—education and law enforcement—are not that complicated. The country did both successfully in the much-maligned

1950s. Schools and criminal justice, following the majority's policies, educated children and maintained law and order at reasonable cost. Indeed, as Sam Francis writes in *Chronicles*: "Most societies in history have never had much of a problem with controlling criminals." It would be hard to find many in America who think children of any race are better educated and trained today then in the 1950s. Violent crime (murder and other non-negligent homicide, forcible rape, aggravated assault, and robbery), according to the FBI Uniform Crime Reports, rose from 288,460 in 1960 to 387,390 in 1965 to 875,910 in 1973 to 1,932,270 in 1992. A *New York Times* poll of June 1994 reports that more than a third of New Yorkers said that, because of their fear of crime, they had moved to new neighborhoods or were planning to. Conceivably, the majority's solutions might have been as feckless as the Court's, but it is hard to believe.

The Court, for a long time, has recognized its power to label something a "constitutional right" and remove it from the political process. Chief Justice Charles Evans Hughes, while governor of New York, said: "We are under a Constitution, but the Constitution is what the judges say it is." Justice Felix Frankfurter wrote in 1958 that "judicial review is a deliberate check upon democracy through an organ of government not subject to popular control." Justice Robert H. Jackson said there was "a basic inconsistency between popular government and judicial supremacy." The will of democracy prevails, in effect, when the Supreme Court says so. In the 1936 decision, *U.S. v. Butler*, Chief Justice Harlan Stone wrote that "while unconstitutional exercise of power by the executive and legislative branches of the government is subject to judicial restraint, the only check upon our own exercise of power is our own sense of self-restraint." The Court's self-restraint proved a slender reed to rely on. The Court, since 1965, has removed great chunks of the public business from the political process.

In any case, a democracy dependent on the self-restraint of judges is not what Madison and Jefferson had in mind. Madison writes that the "fundamental principle of republican government is that the majority who rule in such governments are the safest guardians both of public good and private rights." Democracy assumes a decent respect for the opinions of others, a willingness to accept the vote of the majority, and the ability to compromise. Very few people happily submit to majority decisions they strongly disagree with, but they go along in the hope of being able to change the decision. The theory of democratic consent includes the ability to change the result. In a democracy, as Sidney Hook writes, the appeal from an "unenlightened majority is to an enlightened majority." In Western democracy, the majority allows the minority to enjoy political expression. The minority is granted the right of opposition and consequently the opportunity to become a majority.

Madison and Jefferson were not looking for a system that would find and declare absolute truth; the old world, for centuries, had been ruled by prince and priest in search of that. The people were oppressed and the truth was elusive. The Founders set up a new experiment based upon the sovereignty of the people. The Great Seal of the United States, on the back of the dollar bill, reads above the unfinished pyramid, "He has favored our undertakings," and, at the base of the pyramid, "A new order of the ages." They thought the system would be self-correcting, stable, and allow the most individual freedom.

The Constitution, in fact, is so hard to amend that we had to have a war. Congress, in 1820, enacted the Missouri Compromise that prohibited slavery in any state formed from the Louisiana Territory north of latitude 36°30°N except Missouri. Dred Scott, the slave of a Missouri family sued for his freedom on the basis of having resided for a time in two free areas, Illinois and the Wisconsin territory. The Court, in *Dred Scott v. Sandford* (1856), ruled the Compromise unconstitutional. The Court held that Congress could not ban slave holding in new states because the slave owner had a property interest in the slave that was protected by the Fifth Amendment.

Lincoln did not accept the Court's power; he conceded the Court had the power to dispose of the particular case in front of it but denied it could fix the meaning of the Constitution: "[I]f the policy of the Government upon vital questions affecting the whole people is to be irrevocably fixed by decisions of the Supreme Court the instant they are made in ordinary litigation between parties in personal actions, the people will have ceased to be their own rulers, having to that extent practically resigned their Government into the hands of that eminent tribunal." *Dred Scott*, however, despite Lincoln's opinion, fixed the meaning of the Constitution. It destroyed the existing compromise, and prevented any future political compromise to democratically rid the country of slavery. A war and the Fourteenth Amendment were needed to get *Dred Scott* out of the system. The horrible results of *Dred Scott* show the wisdom of the Founders' insistence on checks and balances. Judicial review, since it makes the Court's decision unreviewable, makes an error likely; also, by centralizing the ultimate decision in the Court, it magnifies the errors that it makes.

Probably, the institution most comparable to the Court is the Papacy. Like the Papacy, the Court determines for itself when it chooses to speak *ex cathedra*, that is, when it will declare a "constitutional right." The Court's declarations, like the Papacy's, are infallible or, at least, unreviewable. Like the Papacy, the losing party has no appeal. The main difference between the two institutions is that the Papacy today has to persuade people that what it declares is really the truth, while the Court's orders are enforced by the coercive power of the state.

The Federal courts now exercise a level of detailed control over public life the Papacy would no longer consider. The courts supervise and, in effect, administer the operation of schools, prisons, mental hospitals, housing agencies, and tax collectors. Ruth Bader Ginsburg, in July 1993, prior to her confirmation hearings, wrote to the Senate Judiciary Committee that federal judges find these "chores" to be "uncongenial and unwelcome." Had "state and federal legislatures" done a better job, she wrote, "the managerial jobs the courts took on, generally with reluctance and misgivings, could have been avoided." The court's reluctance has not prevented them from taking over, by 1993, 80 percent of all state prison systems and about 33 percent of the five hundred largest local jails. Nor does the court's reluctance appear in the language of the consent decrees. The decree covering the Bryce Mental Hospital in Alabama, for example, specifies that "[T]hermostatically controlled hot water shall be provided in adequate quantities and maintained at the required temperature for patient or residential use (110° F at the fixture) and for mechanical dish washing and laundry use (180° F at the equipment)." This kind of detail led Archibald Cox in *The Role of the Supreme Court in American Government* (1976) to conclude that the "individual federal judge became, in effect, the chief executive or administrator of Bryce Hospital."

Similarly, an individual federal judge runs the prison system of South Carolina pursuant to a 1985 consent decree settling a class action brought by the American Civil Liberties Union's National Prison Project. The governor and legislature have nothing to say about it. The 169-page decree specifies the standards for food, clothing, gym, library, square feet per convict, and grievance procedures. The decree further specifies a timetable for rehabilitation and new construction of prisons. It prohibits "triple celling." The state must pay the attorney fees of the ACLU for securing the decree, and any future fees incurred in enforcing compliance with it. If the federal judge believes the state is not complying with the decree he "shall order immediate relief, which may include population reductions including release" of prisoners. Where do the released population reductions go?

Prison systems run by federal judges have a different character from those run by state legislatures. A federal judge in North Carolina, James McMillan, has ordered the state to purchase recreational equipment including three sets of horseshoes, three guitars, five frisbees, fifty decks of playing cards, and a piano. South Carolina, saving itself some legal fees, agreed, without court action, to a recreational program whose stated purpose was "[T]o provide for comprehensive recreational activities for inmates on a voluntary basis reasonably comparable to those available in the community." This includes, but is not limited to "horseshoes, croquet, badminton, [and] paddleball." Regional tournaments are to be scheduled annually for, among other things, "chess, checkers, and backgammon." The backgammon winner of the Regional Tournament goes on to the SCDC [South Carolina Department of Corrections] Championship Tournament unless the "Warden of the host institution" notes a "CAUTION which would prevent the inmate from being transported." Will the released population be able to find competitive backgammon players and appropriate croquet lawns on the outside?

Ruth Bader Ginsburg concludes: "Most urgently needed, I think, is clear recognition by all branches of government that in a representative democracy important policy questions should be confronted, debated, and resolved by elected officials." If they fail, the judges have to fill in the gaps that renders the judge "vulnerable all the more to criticism for excessive or abusive exercise of power." Democracy, according to Justice Ginsburg's theory, means that the elected officials get the first shot at solving problems.

By 1890 America was the wealthiest country in the world. As the wealth poured in the men who created the wealth lost their sense of their proper relation with the rest of the community. The industrialists, in the Hamiltonian tradition, considered man, as Jefferson said, "a beast of burthen made to be rode by him who has genius enough to get a bridle into his mouth." They enlisted the Supreme Court to assist them. The Progressive movement, led by Theodore Roosevelt, was the Jeffersonian reaction to the inequality of wealth created by industrialization.

Theodore Roosevelt and the Progressives came along after the post-Civil War amendments and after the Court's power over the Constitution was solidly established. They understood that meant that most of the Founders' plan was gone—federalism, separation of powers, and checks and balances. They were gone and it didn't look as if they were coming back. The only remaining viable part of the original plan was majority rule. While campaigning in Columbus, Ohio, in 1912, Theodore Roosevelt tried to corral the Court's power. He said, "The people should have the right to recall any decision if they think it is wrong." The Court's power, by Roosevelt's time, had driven the country into another blind alley. Industrialization, following the Civil War, brought David Ricardo's iron law of wages to this country. Ricardo (1772-1823) said that since there is always a surplus of labor and a scarcity of capital, wages will always work down to where they are just enough to keep the worker alive, with a little extra to cover the cost of reproduction. In America, workers stayed at a subsistence level no matter how long, or under what dangerous conditions, they worked. The states enacted laws to limit child labor, hours, and conditions, and to regulate harmful business practices.

How did the Court adapt to the new economic system that replaced Jefferson's agricultural society? The Court enlisted in the cause of capital and threw out all the social legislation. The judicial defenders of *laissez faire* could not, as Sam Francis writes in

Chronicles, resist the temptation of overturning the efforts of Progressive reformers to regulate business at the local level "even at the expense of sacrificing federalism." The Court, to accomplish its goal, invented a new theory called "substantive due process," which it held to from 1890 to 1937, that basically incorporated *laissez faire* economics into the Fourteenth Amendment. The Court may have been right, certainly the country prospered, but it was out of line with the democracy. The Court, as Learned Hand put it, adopted the doctrine that "the court should be the bulwark against" what it considered "improvident, selfish, and uninformed legislation." For example, the Court in *Lochner v. New York* (1905), invalidated New York's Bakeshop Act, a law prohibiting working more than sixty hours in a week, because it interfered with the worker's "liberty of contract." The right to make a contract, the Court said, "is part of the liberty of the individual protected by the Fourteenth Amendment" and the federal courts. Justice Oliver Wendell Holmes, dissenting, said, "I strongly believe that my agreement or disagreement has nothing to do with the right of a majority to embody their opinions in law." The Court overruled the will of the state majority time after time. Holmes dissented time after time. As he wrote in *Tyson & Brother v. Banton* (1927):

> I think the proper course is to recognize that a state legislature can do whatever it sees fit to do unless it is restrained by some express prohibition in the Constitution of the United States or of the State, and that Courts should be careful not to extend such prohibitions beyond their obvious meaning by reading into them conceptions of public policy that the particular Court may happen to entertain.

Theodore Roosevelt thought the court's actions were outrageous. He believed the Court had crossed the line describing its proper role and was openly engaged in allocating wealth and power in American society. He thought the angels had fallen to earth. What could be done to restrain an out-of-control Court? Roosevelt asked why not give the people a chance to overrule the Court after the Court overrules the people? Anytime the Court throws out a law, or whenever it finds a new "constitutional right," the decision is to be put on the ballot at the next general election. The people can decide if they want it or not:

It is the people, and not the judges, who are entitled to say what their constitution means, for the constitution is theirs, it belongs to them and not to their servants in office—any other theory is incompatible with the foundation principles of our government.

Roosevelt's idea, in essence, is a simplified and specific amendment procedure. His idea is necessary to round out Jefferson's theory that each branch has an equal and independent obligation to interpret the Constitution in matters that come before it.   Under Jefferson's approach the Court can interpret the Constitution to decide the case before it. But if the majority disagrees with the Court, it needs some method of instructing the Court of its error. That could be done by the legislature by an ordinary law—as John Marshall himself once suggested (discussed below at 55-56)—but Roosevelt's referendum idea is more coherent with constitutional theory since it allows the people—the source of power—to decide. An expansive Court, under Roosevelt's theory, is met by a simplified amendment process.

As noted, Article V of the Constitution, the present amendment procedure, requires large supermajorities—two-thirds of both houses of Congress to propose an amendment and three-fourths of the states to ratify it. The daunting supermajority requirements made sense when the rest of the 1787 Plan was intact. That is, when we still had those provisions which the Founders designed to limit the power of government to be, as Jefferson said, "energetic"—federalism, checks and balances, and separation of powers. The original idea was to make any change difficult because any change meant more power in government. But with the rest of the 1787 Plan gone and the national Court as the ultimate authority, the required supermajorities have the opposite of the intended effect. Instead of restraining centralized government, they enhance it. The Court, if it has enough support to block an amendment, can grant the rest of the central government power to do what three-fourths of the people don't want it to do. Or it can overrule the way a state or local majority want to handle crime. The minority supporting the Court has to be just strong enough to hold off the amendment process. The beauty of Theodore Roosevelt's plan is that it creates an effective check on the unlimited national government—the national majority.

Roosevelt was the first president to understand the nature of the changed constitutional playing field.   The original contract was fundamentally changed by the Civil War, the Civil War Amendments, and the Supreme Court's allocation of ultimate power to itself through the use of judicial review. Under the original plan, the majority controlled what happened in the country; the local majority controlled what happened in the community; the state majority in the state; and the national majority in the nation. The Civil War finished that system, although its demise was probably not clear until the 1880s and 90s. The Supreme Court had by then made it plain that it would decide basic economic and social policy for the country. An elite, if it could gain control of the Court, could run the country. Roosevelt and the middle-class progressives thought Big Business had done exactly that. A country, however, run by coercive judicial rules and with increasingly great inequalities of wealth can not hold together. The middle class is too small and weak to prevent the extremes from flying apart. Roosevelt's solution was to restore majority rule—the last arrow in the Founder's quiver: The "people should have the right to recall any decision if they think it is wrong." Also, the president, since he represents the national majority, should take a more forceful role than was necessary or appropriate under the old rules. Roosevelt wrote in his *Autobiography*, (1913): "The course I followed, of regarding the executive as subject only to the people, and, under the Constitution, bound to serve the people affirmatively in cases where the Constitution does not explicitly forbid him to render the service, was substantially the course followed by both Andrew Jackson and Abraham Lincoln." John Locke, in his 1690 book, *Of Civil Government*, had the same idea as Roosevelt:

> Who shall be judge whether the prince or legislative act contrary to their trust? This, perhaps, ill-affected and factious men may spread amongst the people, when the prince only makes use of his due prerogative. To this I reply, The people shall be judge; for who shall be judge whether his trustee or deputy acts well and according to the trust reposed in him, but he who deputes him and must, by having deputed him, have still a power to discard him when he fails in his trust? If this be reasonable in particular cases of private men, why should it be otherwise in that of the greatest moment, where the welfare of millions is concerned and also where the evil, if not prevented, is greater, and the redress very difficult, dear, and dangerous?

Jefferson would have liked Theodore Roosevelt's plan. He wrote to Carrington on January 18, 1787: "I am persuaded myself that the good sense of the people will always be found to be the best army. They may be led astray for a moment, but will soon correct themselves. The people are the only censors of their governors: and even their errors will tend to keep these to the true principles of their institution." The constitution, Jefferson thought, should be changed if it could be improved. Jefferson concluded in his 1816 letter to Samuel Kercheval that the Constitution was not an object of worship, "like the arc of the covenant, too sacred to be touched":

> Some men look at constitutions with sanctimonious reverence, and deem them like the arc of the covenant, too sacred to be touched. They ascribe to the men of the preceding age a wisdom more than human, and suppose what they did to be beyond amendment. I knew that age well; I belonged to it, and labored with it. It deserved well of its country. It was very like the present, but without the experience of the present; and forty years of experience in government is worth a century of book-reading; and this they would say themselves, were they to rise from the dead.

Justice Brennan, when he speaks of a "living constitution," means a document that is clay in the hands of the Court. Jefferson's conception of the constitution, on the other hand, is of a document that lives, and changes, in the hands of the people.

Jefferson, in a September 6, 1819 letter to Spencer Roane, wrote that the revolution of 1800 "was as real a revolution in the principles of our government as that of 1776 was in its form; not effected indeed by the sword, as that, but by the rational and peaceable instrument of reform, the suffrage of the people." The nation declared its will "by dismissing the functionaries of one principle, and electing those of another, in the two branches, executive and legislative, submitted to their election."

The revolution, however, was at continuing risk because of the judiciary. Despite twenty years of Republican electoral success, the relentless push of the national court to enhance the national power was "still driving us into consolidation." The people had no power over the judiciary, the "constitution had deprived them of their control." The judiciary, therefore:

> has continued the reprobated system; and although new matter has occasionally been incorporated into the old, yet the leaven of the old mass seems to assimilate to itself the new; and after twenty years' confirmation of

the federated system by the voice of the nation, declared through the medium of elections, we find the Judiciary, on every occasion, still driving us into consolidation.

Jefferson wrote to Thomas Ritchie on December 25, 1820 that it is not the Congress "we have most to fear." The "judiciary of the United States is the subtle corps of sappers and miners constantly working under ground to undermine the foundations of our confederated fabric. They are construing our constitution from a co-ordination of a general and special government to a general and supreme one above. This will lay all things at their feet."

What could rein in the unaccountable judiciary? Impeachment was one possibility. The Constitution called for removal from office for "high crimes and misdemeanors" and gave the House of Representatives the "sole power of impeachment" and the Senate the "sole power to try all impeachments." Senator William Branch Giles of Virginia believed the Constitution did not intend to set up an *independent judiciary*:

> The power of impeachment was given without limitation to the House of Representatives; the power of trying impeachment was given equally without limitation to the Senate; and if the Judges of the Supreme Court should dare, as they had done, to declare an act of Congress unconstitutional, or to send a mandamus to the Secretary of State, as they had done, it was the unreserved right of the House of Representatives to impeach them, and that of the Senate to remove them, for giving such opinions, however honest or sincere they may have been in entertaining them.

Impeachment, Giles argued, "was not a criminal prosecution, it was no prosecution at all," it only signified that the impeached officer's opinions were such that he should be replaced.

Giles' high hopes for the remedy of impeachment collapsed after Justice Samuel Chase of the Supreme Court was narrowly acquitted by the Senate in March 1805. Chase was a turbulent character, a signer of the Declaration of Independence and an opponent of the Constitution, who then turned Federalist. Chase was appointed to the Supreme Court in 1796. Chase presided, as a circuit justice, over several Sedition Act trials in a manner called oppressive, "indecent and tyrannical" by Jefferson's son-in-law John W. Eppes. Chase, in the process of charging a Baltimore grand jury, expressed a few of his political opinions, he said:

> The change of the [Maryland] State constitution, by allowing universal suffrage, will, in my opinion, certainly and rapidly destroy all protection of property, and all security to personal liberty; and our republican constitution will descend into a mobocracy, the worst of all possible governments.

Chase went on to repudiate the Declaration of Independence. It was drafted by "visionary and theoretical writers" (a slightly veiled reference to Jefferson) who believed "that all men in a state of society are entitled to enjoy equal liberty and equal rights." It had brought "mighty mischief" upon the country. Do you have to believe in democracy to be a Supreme Court Justice? After a month-long impeachment trial, the Senate voted 19-15 to convict, which meant Chase was acquitted, since the Constitution requires a two-thirds vote to convict. While the trial was going on, John Marshall, who thought he might be next, offered the surprising compromise that Congress be authorized to overrule the Court rather than remove the judges. Less than two years after *Marbury v. Madison*, Marshall wrote to Chase: "A reversal of those legal opinions deemed unsound by the legislature would certainly better comport with the mildness of our character then a removal of the judge, who has rendered them."

Jefferson, after the remedy of impeachment proved "not even a scare-crow," proposed structural changes to end the independence of the judiciary. In an 1816 letter to Sam Kercheval, Jefferson argued that state court judges should be elected by the people and removable on concurrence of the executive and legislative branches. By 1822 Jefferson thought the Supreme Court had reached a point of crisis: "Before the canker is become inveterate,—before its venom has reached so much of the body politic as to get beyond control, remedy should be applied." One proposal was to turn the Senate into an appellate court on constitutional questions. Jefferson wrote to James Pleasants on December 26, 1821 that he disagreed with that approach since it would allow the Court with half the Senate—representing perhaps a third of the people—"to make *by construction* what they should please of the constitution." Jefferson suggested:

A better remedy I think, and indeed the best I can devise would be to give future commissions to judges for six years (the Senatorial term) with a re-appointmentability by the president with the approbation of both houses. That of the H. of Repr. imports a majority of citizens, that of the Senate a majority of states and that of both a majority of the three sovereign departments of the existing government, to wit, of it's Executive & legislative branches. If this would not be independence enough, I know not what would be such, short of the total irresponsibility under which we are acting and sinning now.

Franklin Roosevelt's New Deal clashed with the Court after it struck down the National Recovery Act (NRA), the centerpiece of the New Deal economic recovery program. Senator Joseph O'Mahoney of Wyoming proposed a constitutional amendment to require a two-thirds vote of the Court to declare an act of Congress unconstitutional. Senator Burton K. Wheeler of Montana proposed one to allow Congress to validate a law declared unconstitutional by the Court with a two-thirds vote of both houses. Franklin D. Roosevelt's "Court packing plan" in 1937, proposed that whenever any federal judge who had served ten years failed to retire within six months after reaching his seventieth birthday, the president could appoint an additional judge to the court on which such judge served. The proposal fixed the maximum number on the Supreme Court at fifteen. The Roosevelt plan was indirect, as constitutional historians Alfred Kelly and Winfred Harbison wrote in 1947: It "dodged the main issue of judicial power upon which so many liberals would willingly have gone forth to battle." Both sides backed away from the constitutional confrontation following extensive hearings before the Senate Judiciary Committee. The Court shifted direction to allow the majority's plans to go forward and Roosevelt abandoned his plans for structural change. Instead, he made over the Court by new appointments. Roosevelt selected nine new angels, second only to the ten chosen by George Washington. Eight of Roosevelt's nine justices had directly served in the New Deal prior to their appointments.

The Court argues that it must retain its unreviewable power so that it can keep the majority from trampling on the rights of an unpopular minority or individual. It is the institution, the Court says, that protects individuals against the majority will. But then where, after 200 years, is the Court's shining case? The case where it stood

at risk to itself, to do justice for an unpopular individual. Indeed, it
has passed up many opportunities. Has the Court just discovered,
say in 1965, that its primary mission is the protection of the individual
against the majority?

A vigorous democracy, according to the Court's theory, is
dangerous for minorities. This is, at best, a peculiar reading of
history. Indeed, the most dangerous form of government for a
minority, judging by modern history, is an ineffectual democracy like
Weimar Germany. The English, who do not have any judicial check
on the majority will, have preserved their individual rights. Professor
Commager wrote in 1943 that "in Britain the people have had the
right to do wrong for some time, now, and have not exercised it in
any notorious fashion." Also, a number of Supreme Court decisions
including *Korematsu v. U.S.* (1944) (Court upholds Executive Order
authorizing military to intern U.S. citizens of Japanese ancestry
during World War II) and *Snepp v. U.S.* (1980) (Court upholds prior
restraint against manuscript of former CIA employee critical of
Vietnam policy even though classified material not involved) show
that the Court's protection may fail when most needed. A security
system that works some of the time, like a difficult car, loses its
charm.

Also, the argument that the Court and the Bill of Rights were
designed to protect a minority from the majority misses the basic
point that any judicial rule binds all. It may be the majority's rule or
the minority's, but it binds all. For example, suppose a town passes
an ordinance against yard signs that the ACLU contests as a violation
of free speech.   Depending on how the Court rules, the yard signs
will be either up or down.   If the Court upholds the town, the
majority rule will bind the minority. If the Court upholds the ACLU
the minority rule will bind the majority. Same with prayer in school,
pornography, flag burning, releasing criminals, and so on. What is a
society like without *any* majority rules? Would the ACLU be able to
live in it?

The Founders were, of course, aware that the majority could be
unjust to the minority. They saw, however, no role for the Supreme
Court to play in the solution to that injustice.   Most
issues—education, crime, and so on—do not carry much likelihood of
oppression, but Madison believed a majority "united by a common

interest or passion" could be expected to oppress the minority. As he wrote to Jefferson in October 1787, the most likely restraint—a "prudent regard to private or partial good, as essentially involved in the general and permanent good of the whole"—should be sufficient, but he did not think it would be: "Experience however shows that it has little effect on individuals, and perhaps still less on a collection of individuals, and least of all on a majority with the public authority in their hands." In *The Federalist* No. 51 he wrote that if the majority is united by a common interest "the rights of the minority will be insecure":

> It is of great importance in a republic, not only to guard the society against the oppression of its rulers; but to guard one part of the society against the injustice of the other part. Different interests necessarily exist in different classes of citizens. If a majority be united by a common interest, the rights of the minority will be insecure.

There are, Madison continued, "but two methods of providing against this evil." One was by "creating a will in the community independent of the majority, that is, of the society itself." This method,

> prevails in all governments possessing an hereditary or self-appointed authority. This, at best, is but a precarious security; because a power independent of the society, may as well espouse the unjust views of the major, as the rightful interests of the minor party, and may possibly be turned against both parties.

A "power independent of the society," like the Supreme Court with judicial review, is, as Messrs. Snepp and Korematsu found out, a "precarious security." The Court may as well support the unjust majority as the rightful minority and "may possibly be turned against both parties."

But Madison did not want a society where the stronger could easily unite to oppress the weaker:

> In a society, under the forms of which the stronger faction can readily unite and oppress the weaker, anarchy may as truly be said to reign, as in a state of nature where the weaker individual is not secured against the violence of the stronger.

Majority rule is not a very attractive system if we are thinking of three people on a desert island and two vote to exploit the third. But that is not the way it works in society. Madison wrote to Jefferson October 24, 1787: "An individual is never allowed to be a judge or even a witness in his own cause. If two individuals are under the bias of interest or enmity against a third, the rights of the latter could never be safely referred to the majority of three. Will two thousand individuals be less apt to oppress one thousand, or two hundred thousand, one hundred thousand?" The second method to secure the rights of the minority is:

> [b]y comprehending in the society so many separate descriptions of citizens, as will render an unjust combination of a majority of the whole very improbable, if not impracticable.
> * * *
> If then there must be different interests and parties in Society; and a majority when united by a common interest or passion can not be restrained from oppressing the minority, what remedy can be found in a republican Government, where the majority must ultimately decide, but that of giving such an extent to its sphere, that no common interest or passion will be likely to unite a majority of the whole number in an unjust pursuit.

The "extent of the sphere" is critical. In a large society, the "people are broken into so many interests and parties, that a common sentiment is less likely to be felt, and the requisite concert less likely to be formed, by a majority of the whole."

This method, Madison said, will be exemplified in the federal republic of the United States in which the society will be broken up into so many parts:

> Whilst all authority in it will be derived from, and dependent on the society, the society itself will be broken into so many parts, interests, and classes of citizens, that the rights of individuals, or of the minority, will be in little danger from interested combinations of the majority.
> ***
> In the extended republic of the United States, and among the great variety of interests, parties, and sects, which it embraces, a coalition of a majority of the whole society could seldom take place upon any other principles, than those of justice and the general good.

Madison foresaw that minorities might seek protection in a "will independent of the society itself," but he warned against it:

> Whilst there being thus less danger to a minor from the will of the major party, there must be less pretext also, to provide for the security of the former, by introducing into the government a will not dependent on the latter; or, in other words, a will independent of the society itself.

Madison's analysis is still good. The American system is broken into so many interests, parties, and sects that there are very few examples of the majority combining to be unjust to the minority. Indeed the problem is the reverse—the risk to the divided majority from a determined minority which manages to ally itself with the governmental bureaucracy. The American majority is so diverse, individualistic, and unorganized that it is easy prey for "those entrusted with the administration" of government.

Madison expected that, if the extent of the sphere was too small, "oppressive combinations may be too easily formed against the weaker party." For example, the Italian City States that were republican in form but oligarchies in practice. On the other hand, if the sphere is too big "a defensive concert may be rendered too difficult against the oppression of those entrusted with the administration."

> The great desideratum in Government is, so to modify the sovereignty as that it may be sufficiently neutral between different parts of the Society to control one part from invading the rights of another, and at the same time sufficiently controlled itself, from setting up an interest adverse to that of the entire Society.

In absolute monarchies, the Prince may be neutral between the different classes of his subjects, but may sacrifice the happiness of all to his personal ambition or avarice. In small republics, the "sovereign will" is restrained from a sacrifice of the entire society, but it is not neutral among the parts composing it.

The Founders thought they had designed the best possible form of government, but whether it would work or not depended on our ability to enlighten the minds of the people at large as Jefferson said, "Enlighten the people generally and tyranny and oppression of body and mind will vanish like spirits at the dawn of day . . . whereas . . .

experience has shown that even under the best form, those entrusted with power, have in time ... perverted it into tyranny ... it is believed that the most effectual means of preventing this would be, to illuminate, as far as practicable, the minds of the people at large." Jefferson concluded: "No government can continue good but under the control of the people."

Does the people's acquiescence in the Supreme Court's assumptions of authority "supply the want of original power"? Jefferson did not think so he wrote to John Pleasants in 1824 that it was dangerous to say to the people "whenever your functionaries exercise unlawful authority over you, if you do not go into actual resistance, it will be deemed acquiescence and confirmation." That was wrong, Jefferson wrote, because "[H]ow long had we acquiesced under usurpations of the British parliament? Had that confirmed them in right, and made our revolution a wrong? Besides, no authority has yet decided whether this resistance must be instantaneous; when the right to resist ceases, or whether it has yet ceased."

"I often wonder," said Learned Hand in 1944, "whether we do not rest our hopes too much upon constitutions, upon laws and upon courts. These are false hopes. Liberty lies in the hearts of men and women; when it dies there, no constitution, no law, no court can save it; no constitution, no law, no court can even do much to help it." "Liberty," wrote Hand, "is the product not of institutions, but of a temper, of an attitude toward life ... [of a] faith in the sacredness of the individual." Courts do not, in fact, act on neutral principles. The spirit of liberty is the "spirit which is not too sure it is right; the spirit of liberty is the spirit which seeks to understand the minds of other men and women; the spirit of liberty is the spirit which weighs their interests alongside its own without bias." Liberty "will prevail only as long as it is supported by the community ... a society so riven that the spirit of moderation is gone, no court *can* save; that a society where that spirit flourishes, no court *need* save; that in a society which evades its responsibility by thrusting upon the courts the nurture of that spirit, that spirit in the end will perish." The ultimate question is whether the rights of individuals are safer in the hands of the majority than in the hands of appointed guardians.

With power goes responsibility. The Court, Professor Corwin wrote, has "made itself morally answerable for the safety and welfare of the nation to an extent utterly without precedent in judicial annals." A free society, wrote Learned Hand, "will find its own solutions more successfully if it is not constricted by judicial intervention." The Court, at will, takes great chunks of public business away from public control. The public, at some point, will have to regain control of its business. "The judiciary," said Hand, "will then cease to be independent" and "its independence will be well lost." The people, after all, are the only ones who can keep liberty in the country.

3

Majority Rule

Sometimes it is said that man cannot be trusted with the government of himself. Can he, then, be trusted with the government of others? Or have we found angels in the forms of kings to govern him? *Let history answer this question.* (Emphasis added)

—Thomas Jefferson, *First Inauguration Address* (1801)

If all power derives from the people, and each citizen is equal and sovereign in this country, it follows that you have to have majority rule. As John Locke put it in *Of Civil Government* "a legislature chosen by the people is the source of all lawful authority, for without this the law could not have that which is absolutely necessary to its being a law, the consent of the society, over whom nobody can have a power to make laws but by their own consent and by authority received from them." The first principle of republicanism is, Jefferson wrote to Baron Alexander von Humboldt on June 13, 1817, "that the *lex majoris partis* [the law of the majority] is the fundamental law of every society of individuals of equal rights; to consider the will of the society enounced by the majority of a single vote, as sacred as if unanimous, is the first of all lessons in importance, yet the last which is thoroughly learnt. This law once disregarded, no other remains but that of force, which ends necessarily in military despotism."

Madison wrote that there is no perfect government or Shining City on the Hill. The will of the majority, the root principle of political democracy, does not remove conflict from the society. But a free

63

government will work out *some* compromise. The only alternative is to take refuge in authority, which is certain, Madison believed, to subvert freedom completely: "that no government of human device and human administration can be perfect; that that which is the least imperfect is therefore the best government."

Majority rule in this country was not firmly established until Jefferson, in his First Inaugural, March 4, 1801, declared that "the will of the majority is in all cases to prevail." Majority rule, since around the 1890s, however, has been eroded by the Supreme Court. Initially, the Court intervened to protect business and capital against state child labor and working condition laws. Since 1965, the Court has intervened to protect various minority interests ranging from criminals to atheists from rules established by the majority. The judicial frustration of the majority will, over time, changed the country's culture. As the Court cut the political process out of most important issues, the significance of that process changed accordingly. The country's resources are no longer at the call of the majority, but are subject to the call of groups who can secure a court order. When the country is running on majority rule, at least 51 percent of the people have to agree on the decision. Judicial rule, on the other hand, selects its winners without respect to popular support. The successful group is rewarded and the rest of the country pays. Majority rule is a naturally unifying principle while judicial rule is a naturally divisive one. Judicial rule breaks down the common will and causes the political process to become an obsolete organ like the appendix. This seems like a very strange point for America to have come to, maybe a look at our history will cast some light.

1774 To 1800

As the Revolution approached, the Founders were becoming less and less humble toward George III. Jefferson, in his 1774 *Summary View of the Rights of British America,* addressed the king, he said, "in the language of truth, and divested of those expressions of servility which would persuade his majesty that we are asking favors, and not rights." Parliament had interfered with the colonists' natural right of free trade with all parts of the world. Jefferson cited the Fur Hat Act to show "with what moderation they [Parliament] are likely to exercise power, where themselves are to feel no part of its weight." According to the act, an American was forbidden to make a hat for himself of the fur which he had taken on his own soil, "an instance of despotism to which no parallel can be produced in the most arbitrary ages of British history." Jefferson told the king, if he was in any doubt about it: "The true ground on which we declare these acts void is, that the British parliament has no right to exercise authority over us." The British Parliament, according to Blackstone's *Commentaries*, was the "supreme, irresistible, absolute, uncontrolled authority in which . . . . the rights of sovereignty reside." No "power on earth", he added, "can undo" an act of Parliament. Parliament made the same point to the American colonists in the 1766 Declaratory Act, asserting that it "had, hath, and of right ought to have, full power and authority to make laws and statutes of sufficient force and validity to bind the colonies and people of America, subjects of the Crown of Great Britian, in all cases whatever."

One other act, Jefferson said, required special mention—an act of Parliament suspending the legislature of New York. Jefferson asked:

> Shall these [state colonial] governments be dissolved, their property annihilated, and their people reduced to a state of nature, at the imperious breath of a body of men, whom they never saw, in whom they never confided, and over whom they have no powers of punishment or removal, let their crimes against the American public be ever so great?

The Parliament passed duties on tea; it provided, in an act for the suppression of riots in Boston, that a person accused of murder, at the Governor's election, would be put on trial in England. Said Jefferson, "cowards who would suffer a countryman to be torn from the bowels of their society, in order to be thus offered a sacrifice to parliamentary tyranny, would merit that everlasting infamy now fixed on the authors of the act."

The king, Jefferson went on, had abused his power to veto the laws of the American legislatures. The abolition of slavery is a "great object of desire in those colonies, where it was unhappily introduced in their infant state." The colonies had repeatedly tried to prohibit further importation, which acts the king vetoed,

> Thus preferring the immediate advantages of a few African corsairs to the lasting interests of the American states, and to the rights of human nature, deeply wounded by this infamous practice.

The king's governors had dissolved state legislatures and refused to call new ones for long periods of time. The legislative power then, Jefferson advised the king, "reverts to the people, who may exercise it to unlimited extent."

Jefferson said we are willing to sacrifice everything which reason can ask for the restoration of tranquility:

> But let them not think to exclude us from going to other markets to dispose of those commodities which they cannot use, or to supply those wants which they cannot supply. Still less let it be proposed that our properties within our own territories shall be taxed or regulated by any power on earth but our own.

Jefferson also suggested to the king that he "[l]et not the name of George the third be a blot on the page of history." The king did not take Jefferson's suggestion, and two years later, Jefferson wrote the Declaration of Independence. On July 4, 1776, George III recorded in his diary: "Nothing happened today."

The Founders were persuaded that their talents and abilities appeared as threats to the King and Parliament. Crane Brinton, in his *Anatomy of Revolution* (1952) writes that one important factor in explaining why a revolution takes place when it does is the "existence among a group, or groups of a feeling that prevailing conditions limit or hinder their economic activity"—a feeling they are "cramped." In America, the Founders were convinced "that British rule was an unnecessary and incalculable restraint, an obstacle to their full success in life."

Jefferson wrote in his draft of the Declaration of Independence: "We hold these truths to be self-evident: that all men are created equal; that they are endowed by their Creator with *inherent* and inalienable rights." He specified that "among these are life, liberty, and the pursuit of happiness: that to secure these rights, governments are instituted among men, deriving their just power from the consent of the governed." He added that "whenever any government becomes destructive of these ends, it is the right of the people to alter or to abolish it, and to institute new government, laying its foundation on such principles, and organizing its powers in such form, as to them shall seem most likely to effect their safety and happiness."

The Declaration, as Joseph Story said, "was an act of original inherent sovereignty by the people." Or, as Jefferson put it in the Declaration, "the legislative powers, incapable of annihilation, have returned to the people at large for their exercise." As John Jay, the first chief justice of the Supreme Court, wrote in *Chisolm v. Georgia*: "From the Crown of Great Britain, the sovereignty of their country passed to the people of it."

Jefferson, of course, did not invent the Declaration's central ideas of (1) human equality; (2) natural and inalienable rights of man; (3) governments created to secure those rights; (4)majority rule; and (5) the right and duty of revolution if government subverts those rights. Jefferson later explained he was not aiming at originality: "Neither aiming at originality of principle or sentiment, nor yet copied from any particular or previous writings, it was intended to be an expression of the American mind, and to give to that expression the proper tone and spirit called for by the occasion." The sentiments expressed, Jefferson wrote in 1819, "were of all America."

Lincoln later noted that the Founders did not mean to say that "[a]ll men were equal in color, size, intelligence, moral development, or social capacity." What they meant was "all men are equal in the possession of certain inalienable rights among which are life, liberty, and the pursuit of happiness."

Government is created by the consent of the governed; that is the only source of power for a just government. What is the nature of the consent and how is it determined? Jefferson's theory of social contract is unique. The traditional view, as expressed by John Locke, starts with an original social compact which is expressed in a constitution. Once the constitution is made, the rights and duties of the citizen and the government are fixed. The constitution can be changed, but not easily and not by a simple majority. John Marshall in *Marbury v. Madison* (1803) said, "The exercise of this original right is a very great exertion, nor can it, nor ought it to be very frequently repeated."

Jefferson, on the other hand, thought the people's consent must be continuing. The original constitution is only an accurate expression of the will of the community for a limited period of time. As a matter of fact, the will of the community changes, and, over time, the original agreement becomes a straight-jacket. Jefferson said: "Laws and institutions must go hand in hand with the progress of the human mind. We might as well require a man to wear still the coat which fitted him when a boy."

The social contract, to Jefferson, was not a historical abstraction; he thought it described the way the American colonies were in fact settled. The Mayflower Compact, the early plantation covenants, and the Revolutionary State Constitutions of 1776-1780 were all examples of actual social compacts. Also, the individual had so much choice as to where he would settle, and he was always free to pick up and move west if he didn't like where he was. So each town, since it was settled by choice, was formed pursuant to a little social contract. Between 1776 and 1780, all thirteen colonies adopted written constitutions establishing social compacts in an independent setting. The Massachusetts Constitution of 1780 provides: "The body politic is formed by a voluntary association of individuals: It is a social compact by which the whole people covenants with each citizen and each citizen with the whole people that all shall be governed by certain laws for the common good."

The necessary change will come one way or another. It may come, as Jefferson and Madison envisioned, when a sufficient consensus among the different elements of society forms to demand it, and thus come about by majority rule. Or it may come when one or more of the parties to the original contract expand their roles. Other parties to the original agreement will have their roles commensurately reduced. The winning parties will justify their expansion by some interpretation of the original contract. This may be acceptable to some of the losing parties, but many will believe their original rights have been usurped. Both sides, in a sense, are right. In the process, however, the society is losing its foundation of consent. Consent is replaced by force and the feeling of many of the citizens that they are being shoved around—which they are.

Jefferson believed there has to be a continuing consent and there are only two ways to provide it: (1) by revolution and (2) by periodic renewal of the fundamental agreement. Revolution and rebellion keep the public spirit alive:

How is it possible for a country to preserve its liberties if the rulers are not occasionally warned of the spirit of resistance among their subjects? What signifies a few lives lost in a century or two. The tree of liberty must be refreshed from time to time with the blood of patriots and tyrants.

Jefferson, on January 30, 1787, wrote to Madison from Paris contrasting the government of our states since the Revolution, "wherein the will of everyone has a just influence," to a government of force like the European monarchies. He found a "great deal of good" in ours. The "mass of mankind under [ours] enjoys a precious degree of liberty and happiness." But, it "has its evils too: the principal of which is the turbulence to which it is subject." He continued:

But weigh this against the oppressions of monarchy, and it becomes nothing. Malo periculosam, libertatem quam quietam servitutem. [I prefer a perilous liberty rather than a quiet servitude.] Even this evil is productive of good. It prevents the degeneracy of government, and nourishes a general attention to the public affairs. I hold it that a little rebellion now and then is a good thing, and as necessary in the political world as storms in the physical. Unsuccessful rebellions indeed generally establish the encroachments on the rights of the people which have produced them. An observation of this truth should render honest republican governors so mild in their punishment of rebellions, as not to discourage them too much. It is a medicine necessary for the sound health of government.

In a free country, a constitutional convention should meet every thirty or forty years to redraft the organic law and submit the result to the people. If the people accept it, it is the new constitution. If the people reject it, the old constitution stays in effect. The fundamental agreement is therefore either renewed or replaced with a new one. To Jefferson, the original contract should last only as long as the original parties. The original parties could, of course, consent to bind themselves. But they had no power to consent on behalf of the succeeding generation: "Each generation is as independent of the one preceding, as that was of all which had gone before." Consent disappeared with the original generation—when more than half of them were gone their old agreement ceased to be based on consent:

It is now forty years since the constitution of Virginia was formed. *Within that period, two-third of the adults then living are now dead.* Have then the remaining third, even if they had the wish, the right to hold in obedience to their will, and to laws heretofore made by them, the other two-thirds, who, with themselves, compose the present mass of adults? If they have not, who has? The dead? But the dead have no rights. They are nothing; and nothing cannot own something. (Emphasis added)

The next generation was like a foreign country which had not consented to anything and was free to do as it wished. Jefferson's study of M. de Buffoun's life expectancy tables showed precisely how long the old constitution fairly reflected the majority will. In the late eighteenth century more than half of those over twenty-one on any given date would be dead in eighteen years and eight months. Today, probably thirty or forty years is close enough.

Jefferson wrote to Major John Cartwright on June 5, 1824:

A generation may bind itself as long as its majority continues in life; when that has disappeared, another majority is in place, holds all the rights and powers their predecessors once held, and may change their laws and institutions to suit themselves. Nothing then is unchangeable but the inherent and unalienable rights of man.

Jefferson, in his correspondence with Madison, recognized that his idea: "[a]t first blush...it may be rallied as a theoretical speculation, but examination will prove it to be solid and salutary." Madison replied that "tacit consent and the failure to revoke could be considered" as agreement. Jefferson disagreed.

Under the theory of judicial review, the Supreme Court is the authorized mechanism for change. Under Jefferson's approach, the people are the mechanism for change. Under Jefferson's theory, judicial review could not get started since there is no need for a specialized tenured body of constitution explainers if the people themselves will explain it shortly. Nor is there any need for lawyers to direct their peculiar code language to the specialized explainers. We would not need the endless empty bitter debate between those who argue for "strict construction" and "original intent" and those who argue for what they call a "living" constitution.

What these two sides are really arguing about is how much change, and what kind of change, the society should have. The two sides, however, are more alike than they are different. They both agree the Supreme Court should direct change in the society. On the other hand, if Jefferson's idea is accepted, the public makes the decision:

> That majority, then, has a right to depute representatives to a Convention, and to make the constitution what they think will be best for themselves. If this avenue be shut to the call of sufferance, it will make itself heard through that of force, and we shall go on, as other nations are doing, in the endless circle of oppression, rebellion, and reformation; and oppression, rebellion, and reformation again; and so on, forever.

A constitution limits the power of the majority. When a majority makes a constitution, or adds a Bill of Rights, it is agreeing that there are things it won't require the government to do during the life of the agreement. It won't ask a president to declare war and it won't ask Congress to suppress disagreeable speech or take property without compensation. It will follow the agreed upon procedures for the expression of the majority will. The purpose of a constitution, Jefferson wrote in his 1781 *Notes on Virginia*, "is to render unnecessary an appeal to the people . . . on every infraction of their rights," on pain that the right will be deemed waived if it is not resisted. Even in the absence of a constitution, Jefferson said:

> I doubt whether the people of this country would suffer an execution for heresy, or a three years imprisonment for not comprehending the mysteries of the Trinity.

But a constitution is necessary, as Jefferson wrote in answer to Query XVII, to bind down the branches of government and to define the spirit of the people:

> But is the spirit of the people an infallible, a permanent reliance? Is it government? Is this the kind of protection we receive in return for the rights we give up? Besides, the spirit of the times may alter, will alter. Our rulers will become corrupt, our people careless. A single zealot may commence persecutor, and better men be his victims. It can never be too often repeated, that the time for fixing every essential right on a legal basis is while our rulers are honest, and ourselves united. From the conclusion of this war we shall be going down hill. It will not then be necessary to resort every moment to the people for support. They will be forgotten, therefore, and their rights disre-

garded. They will forget themselves, but in the sole faculty of making money, and will never think of uniting to effect a due respect for their rights. The shackles, therefore, which shall not be knocked off at the conclusion of the war, will remain on us long, will be made heavier and heavier, till our rights shall revive or expire in a convulsion.

A constitutional system is more stable since it is not necessary to appeal to the people, "or in other words, a rebellion, on every infraction of their rights, on the peril that their acquiescence shall be construed into an intention to surrender those rights."

So there are good reasons to have a constitution, but there is a difficult paradox at the heart of it—the majority agrees to tie its own hands in a way that it cannot undo; they can only be untied by the supermajority amendment process. It has not proven healthy for the majority to keep its original agreement while the Court feels free to interpret a 200-year-old contract as it will. The majority would be happier if it followed Jefferson's idea and came together to make a new contract every thirty or forty years.

The original contract incorporated Jefferson's idea of limited government—government that was so limited in the mission given to it—and the means it was allowed to use—that it could not be very "energetic." He wrote to Madison in 1787, "I own I am not a friend of very energetic government. It is always oppressive." The economic foundation of Jefferson's political system was the self-sustaining agricultural community, as Professor R.R. Palmer writes, "a pre-industrial world of nearly equal property owners, each independent in his own livelihood as a foundation for an equal and democratic society." Jefferson understood that the economically free tend to be politically free, and the economically restricted tend to be politically restricted. As Jefferson's friend John Taylor of Caroline wrote in his 1814 book, *An Inquiry into the Principles and Policies of the Government of the United States*: "Wealth, like suffrage, must be considerably distributed, to sustain a democratic republic; and hence, whatever draws a considerable proportion of either into a few hands, will destroy it. As power follows wealth, the majority must have wealth or lose power."

Jefferson originally hoped that manufacturing would stay overseas, he wrote in 1781: "let our workshops remain in Europe";... "Dependence begatts subservience and venality, suffocates the germ of virtue, and prepares fit tools for the design of ambition." Thirty years later, Jefferson, in an 1816 letter to Benjamin Austin, recognized that "manufacturers are now as necessary to our independence as to our comfort" and "we must now place the manufacturers by the side of the agriculturist."

In the nineteenth century, America became industrialized with the invention and development of railroads, steel mills, electricity, and a national market. The country's workers became dependent on a complicated system of machines and capital. Large inequalities of wealth appeared, endangering the economic basis on which democracy rests. The country, therefore, needed a more vigorous government, such as Theodore Roosevelt's, to balance large private capital on behalf of the citizen. The country, if Jefferson's periodic renewal idea was in place, would have changed the Constitution as soon as the Supreme Court started explaining that the government could not interfere with a child's right to contract to work twelve hours a day. As it was, it took forty years to clear that error from the system. Jefferson believed the current majority is free to change the basic agreement—if they want a more vigorous government they can certainly have one.

The one essential premise of Jeffersonian democracy is the self-governing capacity of the citizen. Jefferson wrote to Dupont de Nemours:

> We both love the people, but you love them as infants whom you are afraid to trust without nurses, and I as adults whom I freely leave to self-government.

Jefferson said in *Notes on Virginia* that the people themselves are the only "safe depositories" of power and "to render even them safe their minds must be improved to a certain degree." On May 26, 1810 he wrote to John Tyler that no republic could maintain itself in strength without general education, "to enable every man to judge for himself what will secure or endanger his freedom." The premise of democracy is that the citizen can make intelligent decisions on the issues before him. As Sidney Hook observed in his *Education For Modern Man* in 1946, educators in a democracy have a greater opportunity and a "greater responsibility for what they do or fail to do, than in any other political order." New ideas get a fairer hearing than in other systems and, most importantly, democracy "permits critical attitudes of thought to develop." Jefferson, of course, thought education critical to the democracy. Jefferson, in *Notes on Virginia* (1781), insisted on universal suffrage:

> The influence over government must be shared among all the people. If every individual which composes their mass participates of the ultimate authority, the government will be safe; because corrupting the whole mass will exceed any private resources of wealth; and public ones cannot be provided but by levies on the people. In this case every man would have to pay his own price. The government of Great-Britain has been corrupted, because but one man in ten has a right to vote for members of parliament. The sellers of the government therefore get nine-tenths of their price clear. It has been thought that corruption is restrained by confining the right of suffrage to a few of the wealthier of the people; but it would be more effectually retrained by an extension of that right to such numbers as would bid defiance to the means of corruption.

American victory in the Revolution, Jefferson wrote in *The Anas*, removed George III but did not settle the issue: "[t]he contests of that day were contests of principle, between the advocates of republican, and those of kingly government, and that had not the former made the efforts they did, our government would have been, even at this early day, a very different thing from what the successful issue of those efforts have made it." The alliance between the states under the old Articles of Confederation for the purpose of joint defense against the aggression of Great Britain was ineffectual in time of peace. Each state returned to being "sovereign and independent in all things." These "separate independencies, like the paltry states of Greece, would be eternally at war with each other, and would become at length the mere partisans and satellites of the leading power of Europe." Consequently, "all looked forward to some further bond of union, which would insure eternal peace and a political system of our own . . . [but opinions divided on whether] all should be consolidated into a single government, or each remain independent as to internal matters, and the whole form a single nation as to what was foreign only, *and whether that national government should be a monarchy or republic.*"

The first efforts to establish a monarchy focused, unsuccessfully, on Washington. Some officers of the army, "trained to monarchy by military habits," proposed to Washington that he assume the crown before disbanding the army. Washington peremptorily refused. Washington told the officers that they could not have found "a person to whom their schemes were more disagreeable" and he directed them, "if you have any regard for yourself or posterity, or respect for me, to banish these thoughts from your mind, and never communicate, as from yourself or any one else, a sentiment of like nature."

The next effort was the establishment of a hereditary Society of Cincinnati, which intended, at some point, to be engrafted on the government with Washington as their head. Washington, after "a whole evening of consultation" with the Society, told Jefferson that he was determined "to use all his endeavors for its total suppression." Washington was not able totally to suppress the Society, but did insist they give up the idea of hereditary membership.

Jefferson and Madison attended the Annapolis Convention in September 1786, which Virginia had called. At this meeting, "a difference of opinion was evident on the question of a republican or kingly government," but the republican view was so general that the kingly "confined themselves to a course of obstruction only, and delay." They hoped that if nothing were done, "all things going from bad to worse, a kingly government might be usurped, and submitted to by the people, as better than anarchy and wars internal and external." The same party used the same practices at Philadelphia to prevent "a government of concord, which they foresaw would be republican, and of forcing through anarchy their way to monarchy."

One of their maneuvers at Philadelphia was the "form of government proposed by Colonel Hamilton." Hamilton proposed his plan as a "compromise between the two parties of royalism and republicanism." The compromise was, however, very unbalanced—the executive and legislative were elected but the executive and Senate were to serve during good behavior, that is, for life. The permanent executive—or elected king—was to appoint the governors of the states, and had the power to veto legislation. When his plan was rejected, Hamilton "left the convention, as desperate, and never returned again until near its final conclusion."

The efforts of the "advocates for monarchy had begotten great jealousy through the States generally," and this jealousy excited strong opposition to the proposed Philadelphia Constitution. Such jealousy "yielded at last only to a general determination to establish certain amendments [the Bill of Rights] as barriers against a government either monarchical or consolidated." Jefferson knew that power corrupts, and that rulers naturally invade the rights of the ruled, as George III did. His solution was to design a government that can't be "energetic"; he wanted a government that was weak, simple, and directly responsible to the people.

"If men were angels," Madison wrote in *The Federalist* No. 51, "no government would be necessary." Or: "If angels were to govern men, neither external nor internal controls on government would be necessary." Madison continued:

> In framing a government which is to be administered by men over men, the great difficulty lies in this: You must first enable the government to control the governed: and in the next place, oblige it to control itself.

Jefferson, in his First Inaugural, noted the lack of angels to govern us saying that sometimes "it is said that man cannot be trusted with the government of himself. Can he, then, be trusted with the government of others? Or have we found angels in the forms of kings to govern him." Subsequently, some other angels have shown up. The current Supreme Court justices, as noted, like the English king, expressly claim the power to govern us. Robert H. Bork, even after he was rejected as an angel, wrote an op-ed piece for the *New York Times*, June 21, 1993, about the need for an increased "American understanding of the Supreme Court's legitimate role in governing us." Bork, in *The Tempting of America* (1990), wrote that the Court is lawless, but we have to have it; the Court is a "great and essential" institution, at page 2, but is guilty of "unprincipled activism," at page 73, and the "usurpation of the democratic authority of the American people" at page 119. It can't be that great and essential if it does those things. Where do these angels—and failed angels—come from?

By Jefferson's account, the early Congresses divided "between the parties styled republicans and federal." The latter being monarchists in principle, of course, adhered to Hamilton as their leader. The Federalists believed in a strong central government, particularly the executive, and the dominance of a social and political aristocracy.

Jefferson's Republican party wanted to (1) keep the legislature pure and independent of the executive and (2) "restrain the administration to republican forms and principals." The written Constitution was not "to be construed into a monarchy" or "to be warped" by the Federalists into "all the principles and pollution of their favorite English model."

The two parties, Jefferson later wrote, "are those of nature." They exist in all countries, he wrote to the Marquis de Lafayette in 1823, "whether called by these names, or by those of Aristocrats and Democrats, Coté Droite and Coté Gauche, Ultras and Radicals, Serviles and Liberals. The sickly, weakly, timid man, fears the people, and is a tory by nature. The healthy, strong and bold, cherishes them, and is formed a whig by nature."

Jefferson believed Hamilton intended to accumulate great power to himself as Secretary of the Treasury. Jefferson wrote to Washington on September 9, 1792 that Hamilton's plan was,

> to draw all the powers of government into the hands of the general legislature, to establish means for corrupting a sufficient corps in that legislature to divide the honest votes & preponderate, by their own, the scale . . . & to have that corps under the command of the Secretary of the Treasury for the purpose of subverting step by step the principles of the constitution, which he has so often declared to be a thing of nothing which must be changed.

The Federalists, with John Adams as president and a majority in Congress and on the federal bench, worked hard to increase federal power. They expanded the size of the army and navy, increased taxes, and passed the Alien and Sedition Laws, designed to cut down criticism of the central government by the Republican press. The Federalists used the prospect of war with France and the horrors of the French Revolution, as Jefferson put it, "as a raw head and bloody bones . . . [with] tales of tub-plots, ocean massacres, bloody buoys and pulpit lyings and slanderings . . . to spread alarm into all but the firmest breast." With their fear of democracy, the Federalists developed a very restricted idea of republican government. As Professor Stephen Presser has written of the Federalist philosophy in *The Original Misunderstanding*: "The people could vote in elections and on constitutions, but once the people had cast their votes, at least according to the Federalist judges, the people were henceforth to refrain from harmful criticism of their properly constituted officials and were to obey them unquestioningly." The Federalists feared that failure to render uncritical obedience to the country's rulers would unleash "the passions and jealousies of the mob." The Federalists were so determined to resist these "passions and jealousies" that they were not above bending legal and constitutional rules. As Alexander Hamilton wrote: "In times like these in which we live, it will not do to be over-scrupulous. It is easy to sacrifice the substantial interests of Society by a strict adherence to ordinary rules." Hamilton's theories anticipate Justice Brennan's fear of the "unabashed enshrinement of majority rule," and he would certainly agree with Justice Brennan that certain questions must be placed "beyond the reach of temporary political majorities." The question was whether the Revolution and the new Constitution would place ultimate sovereignty in the people, as Jefferson advocated, or in some governmental hierarchy resembling the British "mixed" constitution which limited popular influence, as the Federalists hoped.

Jefferson, in his 1823 letter to William Johnson, contrasted the Federalist aims with the Republican:

> To recover, therefore, in practice the powers which the nation had refused, and to warp to their own wishes those actually given, was the steady object of the federal party. Ours, on the contrary, was to maintain the will of the majority of the convention, and of the people themselves. We believed, with them, that man was a rational animal, endowed by nature with rights, and with an innate sense of justice; and that he could be restrained from wrong and protected in right, by moderate powers, confided to persons of his own choice, and held to their duties by dependence on his own will. We believed that the complicated organization of kings, nobles, and priests, was not the wisest nor best to effect the happiness of associated man; that wisdom and virtue were not hereditary; that the trappings of such a machinery, consumed by their expense, those earnings of industry, they were meant to protect, and, by the inequalities they produced, exposed liberty to sufferance. We believed that men, enjoying in ease and security the full fruits of their own industry, enlisted by all their interests on the side of law and order, habituated to think for themselves, and to follow their reason as their guide, would be more easily and safely governed, than with minds nourished in error, and vitiated and debased, as in Europe, by ignorance, indigence and oppression. The cherishment of the people then was our principle, the fear and distrust of them, that of the other party.

But, in the end, the Federalists' tactics failed. As Jefferson wrote:

> For when General Washington was withdrawn, these *energumeni* [demons] of royalism, kept in check hitherto by the dread of his honesty, his firmness, his patriotism, and the authority of his name, now mounted on the car of State and free from control, like Phaeton on that of the sun, drove headlong and wild, looking neither to right nor left, nor regarding anything but the objects they were driving at; until, displaying these fully, the eyes of the nation were opened, and a general disbandment of them from the public councils took place.

In 1800 the Jeffersonians took office and the Federalists began their decline. Jefferson said that he would, by the establishment of republican principles, "sink federalism into an abyss from which there shall be no resurrection for it." The judiciary, however, did not turn over with the election—the Federalists carried on their fight from that safe citadel. The Federalists, Jefferson wrote to John Dickinson on December 19, 1801, "have retired into the judiciary as a stronghold. There the remains of federalism are to be preserved, and fed from the treasury and from that battery all the works of republicans are to be beaten down and erased."

Jefferson's First Inaugural

Jefferson's First Inaugural address, on March 4, 1801, expressed the democratic principle which justified twenty-five years of fighting, first against the Crown and then against the Federalists. The "sacred principle," Jefferson said, was that the "will of the majority was in all cases to prevail." The minority, however, have equal rights "to violate which would be oppression" and the will of the majority "to be rightful, must be reasonable." The minority, after all, after a period of opposition, would often become the majority.

Every "difference of opinion is not a difference of principle . . . we are all republicans—we are federalists." Even those who wish to dissolve the union or change its republican principles should "stand undisturbed as monuments of the safety with which error of opinion may be tolerated where reason is free to combat it." Some honest men fear that a republican government cannot be strong, but will they abandon "the world's best hope" because of the fear? Jefferson believed we are, "on the contrary, the strongest government on earth.

I believe it is the only one where every man, at the call of the law, would fly to the standard of the law, and would meet invasions of the public order as his own personal concern." The country, when men govern themselves, is not perfect. It is not the Shining City on the Hill that the early and modern Puritans are seeking—it is a country as good as the people.

Jefferson asked the citizens to pursue, "with courage and confidence," our own "federal and republican principles, our attachment to our union and representative government." We were kindly "separated by nature and a wide ocean from the exterminating havoc of one quarter of the globe, too high minded to endure the degradations of the others; possessing a chosen country, with room enough for our descendants to the hundredth and thousandth generation."

The country was physically "chosen" and also founded on an idea—that of equal opportunity. We entertained "a due sense of our equal right to the use of our facilities, to the acquisitions of our industry, to honor and confidence from our fellow citizens, resulting not from birth but from our actions and their sense of them." We were also enlightened by a benign religion, "acknowledging and adoring an overruling Providence, which by all its dispensations proves that it delights in the happiness of man here and his greater happiness hereafter."

With all these blessings, "what more is necessary to make us a happy and prosperous people?":

> Still one thing more, fellow citizens, a wise and frugal government, which shall restrain men from injuring one another, which shall leave them otherwise free to regulate their own pursuits of industry and improvement, and shall not take from the mouth of labor the bread it has earned. This is the sum of good government, and this is necessary to close the circle of our felicities.

Toward the close of his address, Jefferson said he was constrained to explain to the people "that you should understand what I deem the essential principles of our government." These are (1) "Equal and exact justice to all men, of whatever state or persuasion, religious or political"; (2) "peace, commerce and honest friendship, with all nations—entangling alliances with none"; (3) "the support of state governments in all their rights, as the most competent administrations for our domestic concerns and the surest bulwarks against anti-republican tendencies"; and (4) "the preservation of the general government in its whole constitutional vigor, as the sheet anchor of our peace at home and safety abroad." His next two essential principles were elections and majority rule. Jefferson, interestingly, considered elections as "remedies"; (5) "a jealous care of the right of election by the people—a mild and safe corrective of abuses which are lopped by the sword of the revolution where peaceable remedies are unprovided"; and (6) "absolute acquiescence in the decision of the majority—the vital principle of republics, from which there is no appeal but to force, the vital principle and immediate parent of despotism."

The other essential principles were more briefly noted: a well-disciplined militia, the supremacy of the civil over the military, economy in government "that labor may be lightly burdened," the honest payment of our debts, freedom of religion, freedom of the press, freedom of the person, trial by juries, and "the diffusion of information and the arraignment of all abuses at the bar of public reason."

These principles form the "bright constellation which has gone before us, and guided our steps through an age of revolution and reformation." They have been attained by the "wisdom of our sages and the blood of our heroes." Should we wander from them in "moments of error or alarm, let us hasten to retrace our steps and to regain the road which alone leads to peace, liberty, and safety."

Most successful revolutions just change the ruling elite; the new group, after a brief period of idealism (in Mexico, this usually involves attempted land reform), goes back to governing a lot like the old group, except often more oppressively. See, for example, the Russian Revolution of 1917. The American Founders, except for Hamilton and a few Federalists, are historically unique in that after winning they did not want to rule. They wanted to go back to what they were doing. They had no love of power and considered government itself to be an evil. Washington could have had all of George III's monarchical power if he wanted it. But he didn't; after he did his duty, he went back to Mount Vernon.

Hamilton, as Washington's secretary of the treasury, worked to undermine the 1776 Revolution by a financial revolution of his own.

An agricultural economy is naturally reflected in the kind of decentralized and weak government that Jefferson wanted. Hamilton had a totally different conception of what society and government should be like. In his 1790 *Report on the Public Credit*, and his 1791 *Report on Manufactures*, he described a great industrial state and an active government. Hamilton believed government was necessary because men required a good deal of control to keep them productive and from harming others—to prevent liberty from being self-destructive, for, as he said in *The Federalist* No. 63, "liberty may be endangered by the abuse of liberty, as well as by the abuses of power." Government was also necessary to create capital. As early as 1779, Hamilton had written to his future father-in-law, Philip Schuyler, that there was not enough money in the country to pay the war debts no matter how effective the tax system was. His solution was a National Bank that would be able to create more money.

The public debt, the federal debt owed to foreigners and the state debts, were a great curse to Jefferson. But to Hamilton it was a public blessing: "A national debt, if it is not excessive, will be to us a national blessing." He persuaded Congress to pay the foreign debt (which was not controversial) and also to recognize the greatly depreciated domestic debts at par and to assume the state debts (which were both very controversial). Hamilton's idea was that the debt, once it was "funded," that is, the interest payments were secured by an appropriation, would be used as money: "It is a well known fact, that in countries in which the national debt is properly funded, and an object of established confidence, it answers most of the purposes of money." Hamilton also proposed a national bank that could issue bank notes and control the economy by expanding or contracting the currency supply.

Hamilton was using financial means to accomplish political and social ends. Jefferson already had a constituency, but Hamilton was creating one. The national bank and protective tariffs built up a moneyed class from banking, shipping, and manufacturing to support the government. A strong central government is necessary for an industrial state. The government has the power, as with a protective tariff, of creating special privileges for certain classes. Hamilton's industrial state meant public debt, military spending, and the tax to support both. His government was necessarily complex and difficult for the ordinary citizen to understand. Hamilton believed the people would prosper under his system and become dependent on it whether they understood it or not. Jefferson, on April 1, 1802, wrote to his secretary of the treasury, Albert Gallatin that a object of great importance was "to simplify our system of finance, and bring it within the comprehension of every member of Congress." Hamilton, Jefferson continued, "set out on a different plan. In order that he might have the entire government of his machine, he determined so to complicate it as that neither the President or Congress should be able to understand it, or to control him. He succeeded in doing this, not only beyond their reach, but so that he at length could not unravel it himself."

The Jeffersonians believed in "real" money, that is, gold and silver, and despised Hamilton's world of speculative paper shuffling, stock-jobbing, and hidden favors. The Federalist goal, Jefferson wrote, was "a single and splendid government of an aristocracy, founded on banking institutions, and moneyed incorporations under the guise and cloak of their favored branches of manufactures, commerce and navigation, riding and ruling over the plundered ploughman and beggared yeomanry."

The Federalists moved to centralize political, as well as economic, power. The Alien and Sedition Laws made it a federal crime to criticize federal officials. The Judiciary Act of 1789 conferred on the Supreme Court jurisdiction not only over lower federal court cases but over state court cases where federal statutes or treaties were involved, or when a state statute or common law rule had been upheld, though challenged under the Federal Constitution. The Supreme Court upheld the validity of the Judiciary Act in the 1816 decision of *Martin v. Hunter's Lessee*. The Court found the power to interpret the Constitution rested with one ultimate source of authority, which was the Court.

Hamilton and the Federalists wanted a strong national state that could rival the great European powers. This meant a strong government, a strong public credit, and a standing army and navy. Professors Stanley Elkins and Eric McKitrick in their 1993 book, *The Age of Federalism*, write that the whole Hamiltonian structure was to be held together, not by republican virtue, but by partonage, interest, ceremony, and force.

Jefferson, after his election in 1800, acted to restore the original Revolution: he abolished most internal taxes, repealed the Alien and Sedition Laws, cut the standing military, and set up a plan to pay off the national debt in sixteen years. Jefferson expected that Hamilton's corrupt "monarchical" system of taxes and elite control would be extinguished with the public debt. Forrest McDonald, in *The Presidency of Thomas Jefferson* (1976), writes that Jefferson's actions defied every precedent: "It was simply not in the nature of government to pay its debts, abolish taxes, deliberately restrict its ability to coerce, or voluntarily reduce its authority; rather the tendency had always been the other way around."

Jefferson's greatest failure, to his mind, was the failure to have *Marbury v. Madison* "denied as law." He wrote to the United States District Attorney for Virginia, George Hay, on June 2, 1807 that "I think it material to stop at the threshold the citing that case as authority, and to have it denied to be law." Jefferson noted that he did not consider himself bound by that decision:

> I have long wished for a proper occasion to have the gratuitous opinion in *Marbury v. Madison* brought before the public, & denounced as not law; & I think the present [Burr trial] a fortunate one, because it occupies such a place in the public attention. I should be glad, therefore, if, in noticing that case, you could take occasion to express the determination of the executive, that the doctrines of that case were given extrajudicially & against law, and that their reverse will be the rule of action with the executive.

Could the American Revolution, renewed by Jefferson, fulfill its promise to better mankind? The theory was now applied to the real world. The country's economic system, after 1801, worked under Jefferson's democratic rules. The democracy's political and economic principles worked together to produce prosperity. The people, free of artificial restraints, were able to develop their talents and abilities to their fullest. Benjamin Franklin did not think it inevitable that America would prosper. He asked what would America be like *without* the Revolution. If we had not had our "timely revolution", we would, Franklin thought, be like the Irish—poor and oppressed.

Jefferson said the people, not the rich, "are our dependence for continued freedom." To preserve the people's independence, he wrote to Sam Kercheval in 1816 "we must not let our rulers load us with perpetual debt." Taxation that follows debt, "and in its train wretchedness and oppression." We must elect between "*economy and liberty* and *profusion and servitude*" (italics in original). Taxes to pay debt service will ultimately push the people to a subsistence level; like the English, we will be unable to afford bread and will have to live, like the English, "on oatmeal and potatoes; have no time to think, no means of calling the mismanagers to account; but be glad to obtain subsistence by hiring ourselves to rivet their chains on the necks of our fellow sufferers."

The Founders' theory of freedom was applied to the new continent and the ordinary man came into his own. Some of the theory went back to Machiavelli, who wrote in his *Discourses* (1521): "It is easy to understand how an affection for living a free way of life springs up in peoples; for one sees by experience that cities have never increased either in power or wealth unless they have been established in liberty." Whenever, he continues, "a tyranny supervenes upon a free way of life . . . it can no longer go forward." It is unable to grow either in power or wealth and usually falls into decline. The reason is that "even if by chance there should arise a tyrannical ruler of real talent and ability, someone who manages by courage and force of arms to increase his dominions, this never results in any benefit to the community but only to the ruler himself." This results because, "not wishing to have any cause to feel jealous of those over whom he is tyrannizing, he will find it impossible to give honorable employment to the best and most valiant citizens." The peoples' talents and abilities invariably appear as a threat to the tyrant.

All countries and provinces, Machiavelli wrote, "that are able to follow a completely free way of life are able to make immense gains." Each citizen "knows not only that he has been born free and not in slavery, but that he can hope to rise by means of his own energies and abilities." The community's wealth grows and multiplies through increases in trade and agriculture. Everyone, Machiavelli concludes, "is willing to increase what he owns and to acquire more goods when he believes that he will be able to enjoy freely what he has acquired. So it comes about that, in emulation with each other, people consider both their own and the public interest, with the result that both the one and the other begin to grow marvelously."

The Tyranny of the Majority

The theory of the tyranny of the majority assumes that the will of the majority and minority rights are antithetical. It assumes that majority rule threatens minority rights and, as Henry Steele Commager wrote, "that the principal function of our constitutional system is to protect minority rights against infringement." It assumes that Jefferson is wrong in believing that the "steady character of our countrymen" expressed through democracy and majority rule is the surest safeguard of minority rights. It assumes that Alexander Hamilton and Justice Brennan are right in believing that it is necessary to have governors who, once given power, are above the wishes of "temporary political majorities," and can avoid "strict adherence to ordinary rules" in order to serve higher "transcendent" values. So plausible are these assumptions, Professor Commager wrote, and "so persuasive is the theory of the tyranny of the majority that many Americans have come to believe that our constitutional system is not, in fact, based upon the principle of majority rule."

Madison, in his essay on factions, *The Federalist* No. 10, wrote that a society with a small number of citizens who assemble and administer the government in person would inevitably fall into the mischiefs of faction:

> A common passion or interest will, in almost every case, be felt by a majority of the whole; a communication and concert, results from the form of government itself; and there is nothing to check the inducements to sacrifice the weaker party, or an obnoxious individual. Hence it is, that such democracies have ever been spectacles of turbulence and contention; have ever been found incompatible with personal security, or the rights of property; and have, in general, been as short in their lives, as they have been violent in their deaths.

By a faction, wrote Madison, "I understand a number of citizens, whether amounting to a majority or minority of the whole, who are united and actuated by some common impulse of passion, or of interest, adverse to the rights of other citizens, or to the permanent and aggregate interests of the community." The latent causes of faction are thus sown in the nature of man:

A zeal for different opinions concerning religion, concerning government, and many other points, as well of speculation as of practice; an attachment of different leaders, ambitiously contending for pre-eminence and power; or to persons of their descriptions, whose fortunes have been interesting to the human passions, have, in turn, divided mankind into parties, inflamed them with mutual animosity, and rendered them much more disposed to vex and oppress each other, than to co-operate for their common good. So strong is this propensity of mankind, to fall into mutual animosities, that where no substantial occasion presents itself, the most frivolous and fanciful distinctions have been sufficient to kindle their unfriendly passions, and excite their most violent conflicts. But the most common and durable source of factions, has been the various and unequal distribution of property.

Where a faction is a minority it can be defeated by regular vote: "It may clog the administration, it may convulse the society; but it will be unable to execute and mask its violence under the forms of the constitution."

However, a faction could well be a majority. How to deal with that, while preserving the spirit and fact of popular government, was the trickiest problem in designing the new government:

When a majority is included in a faction, *the form of popular government, on the other hand, enables it to sacrifice to its ruling passion or interest, both the public good and the rights of other citizens.* To secure the public good, and private rights, against the danger of such a faction, and at the same time to preserve the spirit and the form of popular government, is then the great object to which our inquiries are directed. Let me add, that it is the great desideratum, by which alone this form of government can be rescued from the opprobrium under which it has so long laboured, and be recommended to the esteem and adoption of mankind. (Emphasis added)

The solution to faction, Madison said, was: "Extend the sphere, and you take in a greater variety of parties and interests; you make it less probable that a majority of the whole will have a common motive to invade the rights of other citizens; or if such a common motive exists, it will be more difficult for all who feel it to discover their own strength, and to act in unison with each other. Besides other impediments, it may be remarked, that where there is consciousness of unjust or dishonorable purposes, communication is always checked by distrust, in proportion to the number whose concurrence is necessary."

The Founders, in sum, considered the tyranny of the majority issue, and thought they had answered it as well as it could be answered consistent with self-government. But, almost from the beginning we have heard the complaint that the majority will not treat the minority fairly. Tocqueville, relying heavily on the Federalist Joseph Story, developed the theory of the tyranny of the majority in chapters 15 and 16 of *Democracy in America* (1837). It led him, as it naturally would, to a pessimistic view of the American future:

> Whatever faith I may have in the perfectibility of man, until human nature is altered, and man wholly transformed, I shall refuse to believe in the duration of a government which is called upon to hold together forty different peoples, disseminated over a territory equal to one-half of Europe in extent, to avoid all rivalry, ambition and struggles between them, and to direct their independent activity to the accomplishment of the same designs.

John Adams, in his *Defense of the Constitutions of Government of the United States of America* (1786), wrote that the majority, if not checked, would invade the liberties of the minority: "if you give a [a representative assembly] all the power,—legislative executive and judicial . . . [they will] invade the liberties of the people, at least the majority of them would invade the liberties of the minority, sooner and oftener than any absolute monarchy." What would the majority do? "Debts would be abolished first, taxes laid heavy on the rich, and not at all on the others; and at last a downright equal division of everything be demanded and voted." Anarchy and tyranny commence if it is once admitted that "property is not as sacred as the laws of God." Adams assumed that wealth would always be distributed very unequally, and, consequently, the propertied class would always be a minority and need legal protection.

The voice of the people, Hamilton said, is not the voice of God. Far from it. During the debates at the 1787 Constitutional Convention, Madison records Hamilton as arguing that the rich should have a permanent body to "check the imprudence of democracy":

> The voice of the people has been said to be the voice of God; and however generally this maxim has been quoted and believed, it is not true to fact. The people are turbulent and changing, they seldom judge or determine right.

> Give therefore to the [rich] a distinct, permanent share in the government. They will check the unsteadiness of the second. . . . Can a democratic Assembly, who annually revolve in the mass of the people, be supposed steadily to pursue the public good? Nothing but a permanent body can check the imprudence of democracy. Their turbulent and uncontrolling disposition requires checks.

Later, Hamilton noted, "The people, Sir—the people is a great beast." Jefferson believed the people is not a great beast, but rather a source of democratic renewal. "We of the United States," he wrote, "are constitutionally and conscientiously democrats." As long as "the earth belongs to the living," some "turbulence" is to be expected, and is a good thing.

Hamilton and other believers in enlightened despotism make the critical mistake pointed out by Sidney Hook in his 1962 book, *The Paradoxes of Freedom.* They assume the makers or producers of laws, rather than the users or consumers, are the best judges of their value. The high rhetoric of the guardians crashes on the "homely maxim that only those who wear the shoes know best where they pinch, and in consequence have the knowledge, and therefore the right, to change their political shoes in the light of experience."

Men "need no masters—not even judges," wrote Professor Commager in 1943. Our experience shows that the "majority will does not imperil minority rights, either in theory or operation." The "majority has a vital interest in the preservation of an alert and critical minority and that, conversely, the minority can have no rights fundamentally inimical to the commonwealth." Only in "democracy where there is a free play of ideas," and reconsideration is always open "can there be assurance that both majority and minority rights will be served: "It is the glory of democracy that it—and it alone—can tolerate dissent. It is the strength of democracy that dissent, where tolerated, is helpful rather than harmful."

Jefferson also, of course, believed the majority will was limited; the national majority was limited by the basic compact that delegated to government specific powers. The Alien and Sedition Acts of 1798 were the most oppressive in the country's history. The laws (1) made it criminal for anyone to publish scandalous material about the government or a government official, and (2) authorized the president to imprison or deport any alien he thought dangerous.

Their purpose was to make criticism of Federalist officials dangerous. The federal courts, nonetheless, held the acts constitutional and fined and imprisoned citizens and aliens. John Marshall, while running for Congress from Virginia in 1799, said the acts were constitutional since the "powers necessary for the attainment of all objects which are general in their nature, which interest all America . . . would be naturally vested in the Government of the whole."

Jefferson wrote the Kentucky Resolution of 1799 to call on the other states to join "in declaring these acts void, and of no force." The state legislatures, Jefferson believed, could declare an act of Congress unconstitutional. The national government, he wrote, was created by compact. Jefferson's conception of the Constitution as a compact of sovereign states with the national government as their agent is different from his opinion at the time of his 1787 correspondence with Madison discussed below at 106-107. The resolution declared that the national government "was not made the exclusive or final judge of the extent of the powers delegated to itself; since that would have made its discretion, and not the Constitution, the measure of its powers." If the central government abuses its delegated powers, Jefferson wrote, the members "being chosen by the people, a change by the people would be the constitutional remedy." But where powers are assumed that have not been delegated "a nullification of the act is the rightful remedy." It was argued that the people should have confidence in their chosen representatives and president. Jefferson answered that "free government is founded in jealousy and not in confidence it is jealousy and not confidence which prescribes limited Constitutions to bind down those whom we are obliged to trust with power: that our Constitution has accordingly fixed the limits to which and no further our confidence may go." Let him say what the government is, "if it be not a tyranny, which the men of our choice have conferred on our President, and the President of our choice has assented to, and accepted over the friendly strangers to whom the mild spirit of our country and its laws have pledged hospitality and protection."

By the 1820s, the Jeffersonian Ascendancy had removed most state property qualifications on the right to vote, and the country generally enjoyed universal suffrage for men. In the 1830s, antimajority theory moved from New England—where it was designed to protect property—to the South—where it was designed to protect slavery. The next challenge to "absolute acquiescence in the decisions of the majority" came from the South. John C. Calhoun, in his *A Disquisitions on Government* and *A Discourse on the Government Constitution and Government of the United States*, argued that elections, which Jefferson rested on, did not sufficiently protect the minority. The right of suffrage is inadequate to afford the necessary protection; "it only changes the seat of authority, without counteracting, in the least, the tendency of the government to oppression and abuse of its powers." Calhoun believed there was imminent danger that the majority of the electors will prove to be tyrannical and oppress the weaker minority as intolerably as the most irresponsible government.

The main fault of our system, Calhoun thought, was the despotism of the majority. The majority tends to assume all the rights belonging to the people. Although "only a fraction they assume to be and act as the whole people; while on the other hand the minority is treated as if it were nothing at all." Calhoun framed slavery as a despotism of the majority issue since the essential question was whether the national majority or the regional majority would control.

Madison, after the Constitutional Convention adjourned on September 17, 1787, wrote a long letter to Jefferson summarizing its deliberations. It appeared to be, Madison wrote on October 24, 1787, the "sincere and unanimous wish of the convention to cherish and preserve the Union of the States. No proposition was made, no suggestion was thrown out in favor of a partition of the Empire into two or more Confederacies." With this agreed, the four great objects which presented themselves were:

(1) To unite a proper energy in the Executive and a proper stability in the Legislative departments, with the essential characters of Republican Government; (2) to draw a line of demarkation which would give to the General government every power requisite for general purposes, and leave to the States every power which might be most beneficially administered by them; (3) to provide for the different interests of different parts of the Union; and (4) to adjust the clashing pretensions of the large and small States.

Madison wrote that each of the objects were "pregnant with difficulties," and the Convention's agreement on solutions was nothing "less than a miracle." Of the four great objects, "the due partition of power, between the General and local Governments, was perhaps of all, the most nice and difficult":

> A few contended for an entire abolition of the States; Some for indefinite power of Legislation in the Congress, with a negative on the laws of the States, some for such a power without a negative, some for a limited power of legislation, with such a negative: the majority finally for a limited power without the negative. The question with regard to the Negative underwent repeated discussions, and was finally rejected by a bare majority.

Madison favored the Negative as the best way to overcome the "mortal diseases of the existing constitution." Without it, he said, our system involves the evil of *imperia in imperio* [a government within a government]—some control was needed "by which the general authority may be defended against encroachments of the subordinate authorities, and by which the latter may be restrained from encroachments on each other." Without his Negative, Madison thought it would be impossible to divide the power of legislation between the states and federal government in a way "to be free from different constructions by different interests, or even from ambiguity in the judgment of the impartial". Even the "boundaries between the Executive, Legislative and Judiciary powers, though in general so strongly marked in themselves, consist in many instances of mere shades of difference." Madison's Negative, if adopted, would have made the national majority decisive from the beginning, made the Civil War unnecessary, and short circuited the main purpose of judicial review—the nationalization of power.

Madison discussed the ancient confederations—the Achaen League, Helvetic System, United Netherlands, German Empire, and the United States since 1776. He found them all destroyed, or very weak, because of the "predominance of the local over the federal authority." He recognized that our new Constitution is founded on different principles. It was more like a "feudal system of republics, if such a phrase may be used, than of a Confederacy of independent States." In a feudal system the sovereign, "though limited, is independent, and having no particular sympathy of interests with the great Barons, his ambition had as full play as theirs in the mutual projects of usurpation." And what is to be expected from a feudal constitution?

> In all of them a continual struggle between the head and the inferior members, until a final victory has been gained in some instances by one, in others, by the other of them.

Madison was clear that, without his Negative, which would settle the issue, we could look forward to a continual struggle between the states and federal government until a final victory was won by one side or the other. The virtue of Madison's recommendation of a power in Congress to override or "negative" state statutes was that the ultimate authority would reside in the national legislative branch—Congress. In the absence of Madison's legislative solution, a great deal of power fell into the hands of John Marshall which, as discussed below, he used to the fullest.

The Negative was too nationalistic for Jefferson. He answered Madison on June 20, 1787 that, while he had not thought of it before, he did not like it: "It fails in an essential character, that the hole and the patch should be commensurate." The Negative proposes to mend a small hole "by covering the whole garment." No more than one in a hundred state laws will concern the confederacy but the Negative will require Congress to examine the other ninety-nine to decide they don't. Was there ever a proposition "so plain as to pass Congress without a debate?" It would be better to allow a British creditor denied access to Virginia courts by a state law inconsistent with a Treaty to appeal to the Federal courts. "It will be said that the court may encroach on the jurisdiction of the state courts. It may. But there will be a power, to wit Congress, to watch and restrain them. But place the same authority in Congress itself, and there will be no power above them to perform the same office."

The national court played a critical role in the ultimate victory of the national power. "We find the Judiciary", wrote Jefferson in 1822, "on every occasion, still driving us into consolidation." Jefferson wrote as John Marshall was producing his three major nationalizing decisions. In the first case, *McCulloch v. Maryland*, (1819), involving a state tax on the Bank of the United States, Marshall invented his theory of implied powers to justify Congress in the creating of the bank. The bank was originally chartered in 1791 at Hamilton's suggestion and over Jefferson's objections that it was unconstitutional. Marshall's new theory meant that Congress, in addition to the defined powers the Convention gave it, also had implied powers. Implied powers were those which would, he said, be convenient and helpful in carrying out the defined powers. For example, Congress had the defined power to borrow money, issue currency, support armies, and conduct war, and a bank would be helpful to these, so Congress could make a bank: "Let the end be legitimate . . . and all means which are appropriate . . . which are not prohibited . . . are constitutional." Madison said that Marshall's opinion tended "to convert a limited into an unlimited Government." When the Court's role as ultimate arbiter (*Marbury* and *Hunter's Lessee*) was combined with the flexible standard of what was an implied power (*McCulloch*), the Court became the ultimate arbiter of what Congress could do. The Virginia legislature repudiated implied powers and recommended a constitutional amendment. Ohio went further and, in effect, nullified the decision by sending its tax officials into the vaults of the Bank's Ohio branch to collect the $100,000 tax.

In the second case, *Cohens v. Virginia*, (1821) Marshall proved that the most clear language of a constitutional amendment could not bind the Court. The Eleventh Amendment was adopted 1798 to overrule a earlier Supreme Court decision which held that a State could be sued in a federal court. The Eleventh Amendment said that a state could not be sued without its consent, specifically, that the judicial power of the United States shall not be construed to extend to any suit "commenced or prosecuted against one of the States." Virginia believed the language was conclusive and meant that *Cohens* could not bring the State into a federal court. Marshall, however, found that the Court had jurisdiction over Virginia. The clear language of the amendment, he believed, need not be read literally because he understood the purpose of the amendment was more limited. Here, Marshall combined his ultimate arbiter role with the power to construe words to mean something different than the language used, that is, "shall not be construed to extend" may be construed to mean "shall be construed to extend." In *Cohens* and *Hunter's Lessee*, Marshall used the Constitution, in Jefferson's words, as a "mere thing of wax" to establish that the federal system would operate under one supreme law, and that the Supreme Court was the ultimate arbiter of that law.

Marshall, as he was reworking the Constitution, threw in some attacks on Jefferson, whom he called "the Great Llama of the Little Mountain." Jefferson did not return the personal attacks, but did write to Thomas Ritchie in 1820 that the nation's attention should be drawn "to these bold speculators on its patience." He also wrote to Virginia Senator Nathaniel Macon that the Marshall-led Court was "the germ of dissolution of our federal government" and "an irresponsible body" working "like gravity, by day and night, gaining a little today and a little tomorrow, and advancing its noiseless step, like a thief over the fields of jurisdiction, until all shall be usurped from the States, the government of all becoming a consolidated one."

The third Marshall opinion, *Gibbons v. Ogden* (1824), was less controversial but equally far reaching. The Court struck down New York's law which closed the state's ports to steamships not owned or licensed by a monopoly chartered by the state for the benefit of Robert Fulton. New Jersey and Connecticut passed retaliatory acts closing their ports to the New York boats. Gibbons operated a steamship in defiance of the monopoly between Elizabethtown, New Jersey and New York City. New York seized and condemned his vessel. Marshall overturned the New York law. The Constitution expressly gave Congress the power to regulate interstate commerce to provide for free trade among the states, so while Marshall gave the power a broad construction, he did not invent the power or give the words unintended meaning. *Gibbons v. Ogden* did not therefore set off the firestorm that *McCulloch*, and *Cohens,* and *Hunter's Lessee* had.

Jefferson, in 1822, wrote that Marshall and the Federalists, like "the fox pursued by the dogs...take shelter in the midst of the sheep. They see that monarchism is a hopeless wish in this country, and are rallying anew to the next best point, a consolidated government." In the same year Jefferson wrote to William Johnson: "I scarcely know myself which is most to be deprecated, a consolidation or dissolution of the states. The horrors of both are beyond the reach of human foresight."

The message of Marshall's opinions was clear enough to Calhoun. "Who are to judge," Calhoun asked Webster on February 26, 1833, "whether the laws be or be not pursuant to the Constitution?" If the departments of the national government "are to possess the right of judging, finally and conclusively, of their powers, on what principle can the same right be withheld from the State Governments." Judicial review, by the time of the 1830 Senate debates, (January 20-21, 29 and February 4-8) was a central issue in the slavery debate. Daniel Webster of Massachusetts argued that the exclusive right of deciding constitutional disputes resided in the Supreme Court. Thomas Hart Benton of Missouri denied the Court had any exclusive right; that would be "a despotic power which would lead inexorably to "the annihilation of the States." Benton was joined by John Rowan of Kentucky, who said the claimed exclusive authority of the Court was an "irresponsible" power not intended by the framers of the Constitution and wholly inconsistent with the American tradition of self-government. Such a power would lead ineluctably to "judicial tyranny" and unchecked federal usurpation. The Southern Senators understood, that if judicial review was accepted, in the long run they had to lose. The national court, over time, would expand the national jurisdiction.

The South proposed that the constitutionality of federal laws should be decided by state nullification. Senator Felix Grundy of Tennessee, on February 29, 1830, said that a state could nullify a federal law and yet remain in the union. After remonstrance and protest failed, said Grundy, a state could call a state convention for the purpose of nullifying the federal law. The federal government, if the state convention voted to nullify, had two options: (1) repeal the law or (2) call a convention of the states to ask for an amendment sanctioning the power. The ultimate arbiter of the Constitution would then, Grundy said, be the "the people of the Union, assembled by their deputies in Convention."

Calhoun—unlike Jefferson—believed that democracy could exist despite large inequalities. He wrote that slavery "forms the most solid and durable foundation on which to rear free institutions." Indeed, he thought slavery enhanced democracy. Look at Athens, he said: those who perform the labor and menial duties in the society do not have the leisure necessary for political observation and reflection. They lower the democratic average for the society since they are not qualified to perform their democratic duties. A very fine democracy, on the other hand, could exist among the members of the ruling class who have the time and capacity to perform their democratic duties. We would have fewer, but better, democrats.

Calhoun was trying to develop a theory for a democratic conundrum—a perpetual minority—one that never will have a remedy in an election. Usually, the minority in a democracy will shift with the issue. The same citizen will be with the majority on a number of issues, and even when he is in the minority, can hope to change some minds and turn the minority into a majority. Calhoun's minority could not expect to do that. Calhoun's solution was the "concurrent majority by which the majority could not act unless various interests" (minorities) agreed with the decision. Aside from the practical difficulty of determining what interests get the veto power, it is clear that Calhoun's democracy is not Jefferson's. Calhoun was trying to do something that cannot be done—where a minority is culturally distinct (e.g., pre-Civil War Southerners, Mormons), and is always going to be a minority, Jeffersonian elections will not help except to provide an education system that will enable the minority to develop its talents. But there is no way, consistent with Jefferson's view, for the minority to impose its beliefs on the majority.

A hundred and fifty years after Calhoun, Lani Guinier, a Pennsylvania Law School Professor, in *The Tyranny of the Majority: Fundamental Fairness in Representative Democracy* (1994), adopted Calhoun's theories to benefit the descendants of the slaves rather than the slave-owners. Ms. Guinier, like Calhoun, starts with the proposition that democracy and majority rule are not the same thing. Both think democracy is consistent with supermajority requirements that require more than a 51 percent vote for a law to pass. They also agree that voting is a group right, not an individual right, and that the interest group is what should be represented. They also have the same problem, to fairly say which group will get special protection—will it be beer drinkers, cigar smokers, and T.V. football addicts? Is that three groups or one? American democracy, Ms. Guinier believes, is an extreme form of what she calls "winner take all" majority rule. She contrasts it to Israel, which gives a seat to any party that can get a one percent vote. She believes, like Calhoun, that a majority rule system means the 51 percent will take 100 percent of the power and exploit the 49 percent, or as she puts it: "Any form of less than unanimous voting introduces the danger that some group will be in the minority and the larger group will exploit the numerically smaller group." The majority will enact laws against "blacks, [who] as a poor and historically oppressed group, are in greater need of government-sponsored programs and solicitude." A better political system, she believes, will "insure that disadvantaged and stigmatized groups also have a fair chance to have their policy preference satisfied." She believes racial minorities have made "a strong, historically supported and congressionally mandated case for their claims that a homogenous, permanent majority has exercised disproportionate power consistently to degrade their influence on the political process as a whole." But if the "homogenous, permanent majority" is so oppressive, how did the minorities get their claims "congressionally mandated"?

Ms. Guinier recommends cumulative voting, proportional representation and supermajority voting as mechanisms to give the minority increased bargaining power, if not a veto power. Ms. Guinier, like Calhoun, goes off the track right at the beginning—voting is the individual's right, not a group right. President Clinton, on April 29, 1993 nominated Ms. Guinier, to be assistant attorney general for civil rights. Five weeks later, on June 3, 1993, he withdrew her nomination.

The minority's options in a non-Calhoun-Guinier world are those discussed in chapter 1: they can accept what the majority has relegated them to, try to change the majority's mind, leave, or revolt. Calhoun and the southern states argued that their beliefs were majority beliefs in their states and region; that is, they only became a minority if you considered the nation as a whole. Like the Protestants in Northern Ireland, they are a majority in their section, but in Ireland as a whole, they are a tiny minority. The issue of where the boundary will be drawn is outside of democratic theory, and is usually settled by force or the threat of force. For example, in Bosnia, the Muslims drew the boundaries of their newly created state to include a 30 percent Catholic and Orthodox population—who did not agree to be included—which has led to a violent redrawing of the boundaries.

Jefferson, in the First Inaugural, admonished the majority that, to be "rightful," it must be "reasonable"; that minorities "possess their equal rights," which to violate would be "oppression." And, as he said later in the same address, there must be "an absolute acquiescence in the decisions of the majority." Jefferson wrote to Madison on December 20, 1787: "after all, it is my principle that the will of the majority should always prevail." So, in the last analysis, the majority decides what is "reasonable." If it oversteps fairness, it becomes an oppressive majority; and the wronged minority has the same natural right remedy the colonists had in the Revolution—if a government pursues a long train of abuses and usurpations, "it is their right, it is their duty to throw off such government." This right, Madison said, was not a legal right but a natural right; it did not come from the Constitution, but from the abuses or usurpations which released the "parties to it from their obligation."

The tyranny of the majority theory of Adams, Tocqueville, Calhoun, and Guinier rests on the premise that the majority will not treat the minority fairly. They believe the majority will should be checked by some means, perhaps by "concurrent power," or perhaps by judicial review. Some check is needed to preserve the minority's property and civil liberties. If, however, we do not trust the majority to be fair in these critical areas, why should we trust it at all? As Madison wrote: "If the will of the majority cannot be trusted where there are diversified and conflicting interests, it can be trusted nowhere, because such interests exist everywhere."

Democracy, of course, fails if we don't trust the majority. Jefferson wrote Madison from Paris on January 30, 1787 concerning "the late troubles in the Eastern states." He hoped those in power would not overreact. He feared that "[t]hey may conclude too hastily that nature has formed man insusceptible of any other government but that of force, a conclusion not founded in truth, nor experience."

Jefferson wrote to David Hartley on July 2, 1787:

> I have no fear that the result of our experiment will be that men may be trusted to govern themselves without a master. Could the contrary of this be proved, I should conclude either that there is no god, or that he is a malevolent being.

What about term limits? A lot of good people support them as a way to restrain an out-of-control Congress but the Founders decided against them, and left out of the Constitution what was then called rotation. They thought it would allow the representative to ignore the voters. For example, Madison, in *The Federalist* No. 57, wrote that frequent elections are necessary to tie the representatives to the people. The representative will quickly forget his dependence once he is in office and exercising power; he will forget where he came from.   Elections every two years will compel the members "to anticipate the moment when their power is to cease, when their exercise of it is to be reviewed, and when they must descend to the level from which they were raised; there forever to remain unless a faithful discharge of their trust shall have established their title to a renewal of it." A representative in his last term under a term limit law, however, is free to ignore his constituents. They have no control over him.

George Will, in *Restoration* (1992), writes that "something must be done to restore Congress to competence and respect, and that term limits can do it." Assuming the first part can be done, how will term limits do it? Will says it will by breaking up the "permanent class of career legislators." But, according to the *New York Times* of May 15, 1994, that class is already broken up; it is almost certain that more than half the members of the House that convenes in January 1995 will have served four years or less.

Term limits, according to Will's bookjacket, will restore "the healthy distance between the electors and the elected that is necessary for genuine deliberation about the public interest." His model is Edmund Burke who told his Bristol constituents in 1774, *after they had elected him*, that he did not owe them obedience and need not follow their instructions; his obligation to them was to exercise his judgment—about ends as well as means. That is a little haughty for America. Madison and the Founders did not believe representatives should be independent of their constituents. They should not exercise power in the people's name unless they are subject to the people's sanctions.   Will believes that today's representatives are "like puppies on very short leashes that are held by very short-tempered masters." But every poll shows the people do not feel like masters, and they are not getting anything near what they want from Congress. And what puppy ever voted himself a pay raise?

The Earth Belongs to the Living—Continuing Consent

The basic democratic question is how much power the current majority has. Theoretically, it has a great deal of power. But under contemporary American practice, the current majority has very little free play—25 percent of total government revenues or 50 percent of individual and corporate income taxes—go to pay interest on past debts. The interest must be paid before the government can buy a peanut butter sandwich. Nor can the majority—by majority vote—change the Supreme Court's decisions or change the Constitution to limit the Court's power. Jefferson thought the current majority could never get itself into such a pitiful situation—each generation has the power, morally and legally, to recreate the state by a new constituent convention and written constitution.

Jefferson's theory of debt is one example of his basic premise that one generation cannot bind another: "No generation can contract debts greater than may be paid during the course of its own existence." The "*earth belongs in usufruct* [trust] *to the living* . . . the dead have neither powers nor rights over it" (emphasis added). If one generation can charge another for its debts, "then the earth would belong to the dead and not to the living generation." Jefferson continued: "The conclusion then, is, that neither the representatives of a nation, *nor the whole nation itself assembled,* can validly engage debts beyond what they may pay in their own time" (emphasis added).

Arphaxad Loomis, at New York's 1846 Constitutional Convention, expressed the Jeffersonian belief that one generation cannot bind another without its consent:

> The legislature and the people—never had the right to legislate for the future, to enthrall and bind down those who come after them either by debt or any other system of legislation which would prevent them from a perfect freedom of action.

Jefferson believed the principle that one generation cannot bind another is morally correct and is also, more importantly, a simple statement of fact. No current decision irrevocably binds future generations. The earth does belong to the living, the subsequent generation cannot be bound by a past one; the future always does have a perfect freedom of action whether they realize it or not. Chains, as Jefferson wrote, are always self-imposed.

The chains on the current majority are primarily two: (1) a perpetual unpayable debt, and (2) a Supreme Court with the ultimate say on basic political, economic, and social issues. Jefferson would consider both of these chains to be self-imposed. The present generation, for example, is not responsible for what might be called the "Louis XV debt." Jefferson wrote:

> Again suppose Louis XV and his contemporary generation had said to the money-lenders of Genoa, give us money that we may eat, drink, and be merry in our day; and on condition you will demand no interest till the end of 19 years you shall then for ever after receive an annual interest of 12-5/8 per cent. The money is lent on these conditions, is divided among the living, eaten, drank, and squandered. Would the present generation be obliged to apply the produce of the earth and of their labor to replace their dissipations? Not at all.

New York's 1846 Constitutional Convention applied Jeffersonian principles to distinguish the wasteful debt of Louis XV to the Genoese bankers and debt used to construct canals, roads, and other productive projects. Debt could make a country function better; for example, how much better off would the people of Russia be if they had better highways, rails, and airports? The future could justly be asked to pay if the debt was incurred to benefit the future. But the power to borrow is the most dangerous power a democracy can have—a bad law can be repealed but a bad debt cannot be. The convention's solution was to require, before the state could incur any debt, a specific vote of the people to approve the debt and also, at the same time, to impose a new tax sufficient to pay it off in eighteen years. The convention believed the requirement of a new tax would give reasonable security against unnecessary and improper debt. The new tax approach is a practical way of accomplishing Jefferson's theory of legitimate debt:

Funding I consider as limited, rightfully, to a redemption of the debt within the lives of a majority of the generation contracting it; every generation coming equally, by the laws of the Creator of the world, to the free possession of the earth he made for their subsistence, unincumbered by their predecessors, who, like them, were but tenants for life.

The Founders—other than Hamilton—believed the democracy could not tolerate a perpetual public debt.   Washington, on November 19, 1794, urged Congress to provide "a definitive plan for the redemption of the Public Debt." Hamilton proposed funding the debt over thirty years with surplus tariff revenues and a special excise tax.   Madison said thirty years was too long: "a debt which will require more than 30 years (the term calculated) [by Hamilton] to pay it off, *will never be paid*" (emphasis added). New emergencies will add to it faster than the debt is reduced. Madison recommended a direct property tax apportioned among the states.   However, a federal property tax was not imposed, and the country did not get out of debt until Andrew Jackson's administration. The object of the debate remained: how to confine the debt-making power so that it does not contradict democracy by binding future unrepresented generations.

Debt is essentially antidemocratic, because it restrains the freedom of future generations without their consent. Jefferson believed that economic democracy is inseparable from political democracy.   In a democracy you have to agree on what you want to do and on how to pay for it.   A pay-as-you-go system demands immediate taxes to cover all spending. What the payees will currently receive, the payers must currently pay; the payers are apt to resist, the issue must be discussed, and some compromise reached. With a borrowing policy, Jefferson said, the rules are entirely different. Debt, since it requires no immediate taxes, separates the recipient from the payer.   The future taxpayer, who will pay, is not represented by any of the current parties.   The burden is easily cast upon the unrepresented future. This is the real tyranny of the majority, the tyranny of the current majority over the future majority. Spending money, Jefferson said, "to be paid by posterity under the name of funding is but swindling futurity on a large scale."

Madison believed war to be the most dreaded public enemy since it led to debt. He wrote, in 1795, "of all the enemies to public liberty, war is, perhaps, the most to be dreaded, because it comprises and develops the germ of every other. War is the parent of armies; from these proceed debts and taxes; and armies, and *debts, and taxes are the known instruments for bringing the many under the domination of the few"* (emphasis added). The fore horse of this frightful team, Jefferson wrote in 1816, "is public debt. Taxation follows that, and in its train wretchedness and oppression." The society is reduced to be "mere automatons of misery, and to have no sensibilities left but for sinning and suffering." Then begins the *bellum omnium in omnia* (the war of all against all).

Jefferson noted that England, under George III, had alienated the whole island to its creditors:

> George the III in execution of the trust confided to him, has, within his own day, loaded the inhabitants of Great-Britain with debts equal to the whole fee-simple value of their island, and under pretext of governing it, has alienated its whole soil to creditors who could lend money to be lavished on priests, pensions, plunder and perpetual war. This would not have been so, had the people retained organized means of acting on their agents. In this example, then, let us read a lesson for ourselves, and not "go and do likewise."

The citizen's right to be free of the prior generation's debt, Jefferson said, "like some other natural rights...has not yet entered into any declaration of rights, it is no less a law, and ought to be acted on by honest governments." It would be, Jefferson wrote to John Eppes in 1813, "a salutary curb on the spirit of war and indebtment, which, since the modern theory of the perpetuation of debt, has drenched the earth with blood, and crushed its inhabitants under burthens ever accumulating."

Debt, Jefferson believed, always concentrated power in an elite; debt meant more taxes to pay it and more government to handle it. He wrote to John Taylor, on November 26, 1798: "I wish it were possible to obtain a single amendment to our Constitution. I would be willing to depend on that alone for the reduction of the administration of our government to the genuine principles of its Constitution. *I mean an additional article, taking from the federal government the power of borrowing"* (emphasis added).

The federal government will, of course, lose the power to borrow when it is no longer creditworthy, that is, when no one will lend to it.

We intuitively view this as a cataclysmic disaster, and it may well be under present circumstances. But Jefferson looked forward to the loss of the national credit. He wrote to A. Stuart in 1786: "Good will arise from the destruction."

Jefferson wrote to Nathaniel Macon on August 19, 1821 that "there are two measures which if not taken, we are undone." The first was to check, as previously discussed, the "unconstitutional invasions" by the Supreme Court. The second was:

> To cease borrowing money & to pay off the national debt. If this cannot be done without dismissing the army & putting the ships out of commission, haul them up high and dry, and reduce the army to the lowest point at which it was ever established. There does not exist an engine so corruptive of the government and so demoralizing of the nation as a public debt. It will bring on us more ruin at home than all the enemies from abroad against whom this army and navy are to protect us.

The Senate, on March 1, 1994, rejected the Balanced Budget Amendment by a Senate vote of 63-37—a two-thirds vote is needed. Senator Robert Byrd of West Virginia said the amendment would "undermine democracy"—the right to run a deficit which the Founders had given us. Can you fail to balance the budget *forever*?

The present majority is not bound by the debt anymore than it is bound by the Court's explanation of the Constitution. The current majority is bound by moral—not legal—principles: it should behave "rightfully" to the minority, and it should recognize that it holds the earth in trust for the future. Jefferson would agree with Theodore Roosevelt's First Message to Congress:

> If in a given community unchecked popular rule means unlimited waste and destruction of natural resources—soil fertility, water-power, forests, game, wild life generally which by right belongs as much to subsequent generations as to the present generation than it is a sure proof that the present generation is not yet really fit for self control.

Both Roosevelt and Jefferson believe the present majority has the power to deal with its problems, and with full knowledge of the facts, will come to the best decision.

David Hume wrote that history did not factually support the idea that the majority of the people were sovereign. Hume said Locke and Jefferson were inventing a fictional world—government is not formed by a contract under which the governed agree to obey and the governors agree to stay within the terms of the contract. Government, Hume said, is mostly formed in fraud and force, and it is obeyed "because society could not otherwise subsist." Jefferson responded sharply. In a letter to John Cartwright in June 1824, he wrote "And where else will this degenerate son of science, this traitor to his fellow men, find the origin of just powers, if not in the majority of the society? Will it be in the minority? Or an individual of that minority." Jefferson thought of democracy not primarily as a political issue, but as the liberation of the human spirit from imposed and self-imposed chains. The imposed chains were broken by limited government which got rid of kings and judges who held discretionary power over the people. The self-imposed chains are to be broken by education, reason, and truth.

Next to debt, the biggest chain on the current majority is the 1787 Compact as interpreted by the Supreme Court. Jefferson did not have any reverence for the Constitution. As he said, he knew the Founders, and they were fine people, but quite human. He did not "look at the constitutions with sanctimonious reverence and deem them like the ark of the covenant, too sacred to be touched."

Jefferson's theory of the nature of consent is unique. The traditional theory of John Locke has the people forming a social compact which, once made, they are permanently committed to and can only amend with great effort. We are following Locke when the Court tries to interpret a 1787 Constitution. Jefferson's theory is totally different—each generation is to establish its own law. It made him tolerant of revolution. For example, he wrote of Shay's Rebellion that it was better for them to take up arms than tamely submit. It made him propose a periodic renewal of the basic agreement. Jefferson insisted on a real new agreement; he disagreed with Madison that a tacit or implied consent could be read in if there was a failure to alter or revoke the old agreement. Jefferson replied that he might agree if the "will of the majority could always be obtained fairly and without impediment":

> It might be indeed if every form of government were so perfectly contrived that the will of the majority could always be obtained fairly and without impediment. But this is true of no form. The people cannot assemble

themselves. Their representation is unequal and vicious. Various checks are opposed to every legislative proposition. Factions get possession of the public councils. Bribery corrupts them. Personal interests lead them astray from the general interests of their constituents: and other impediments arise so as to prove to every practical man that a law of limited duration is much more manageable than one which needs a repeal.

Jefferson noted that, first, the Constitution, as adopted, does not allow for alteration or revocation by majority vote. Second, he thought that all the foundation principles should be thought through and agreed to again by each generation. In a convention, the people, as Peter R. Livingston told the 1821 New York Constitutional Convention, "are here themselves":

No restriction limits our proceedings. What are these *vested* rights? Sir, we are standing upon the foundations of society. The elements of government are scattered around us. All rights are buried; and from the shoots that spring from their grave we are to weave a bower that shall overshadow and protect our liberties.

Each generation, then, makes its own agreement. Otherwise, if the constitution "be enforced longer, it is an act of force and not of right." A side benefit of Jefferson's continuing consent theory is that it eliminates any excuse for judicial review. The wisdom and mystery of the Supreme Court is not necessary to interpret a Constitution we drafted in 1965 and which we are going to change in 1995 anyway.

In one sense, Jefferson's theory just formalizes what is going to happen anyway. A succeeding generation, as a matter of fact, is not going to be shackled by the past. A succeeding generation will change the original compact to suit its situation. The expansion of national power, the deletion of federalism, the elimination of the separation of powers, the unlimited taxing power, all well accepted today, obviously do not conform to the original compact's idea of limited government. There is no question the change had to come. What is unfortunate is that we have used the Court as the vehicle for change. This has encouraged it to think of itself in large—and undemocratic—terms. That malevolent genie has not been put back in the bottle yet. If, on the other hand, we had done it Jefferson's way, the means of change would have been the constituent convention followed by a vote of the people. Certainly that would have been better.

The dust jacket for a recent book, Ronald Dworkin's *Life's Dominion*, explains that the Constitution "is inescapably a set of abstract moral principles that must be reinterpreted, generation by generation." Mr. Dworkin believes the Supreme Court, since it is appointed by elected officials, should carry on the job of periodic reinterpretation. Inescapably or not, Jefferson would disagree with all three of the author's propositions: (1) the Constitution is not a set of abstract moral principles; (2) it should not be reinterpreted generation after generation; and (3) if that were to be done, the justices are not the ones to do the job.

Mr. Dworkin believes the justices are angels sent here to govern us. In a recent review of Gerald Gunther's book, *Learned Hand: The Man and the Judge* (1994) Dworkin puts what he correctly calls the "inescapable question": "whether, in the end, the interpretations of the legislatures or those of the judges will prevail, and though lawyers who dislike either answer call for something in between, there is, as Hand pointed out, no logical space for anything in between." Hand, Jefferson, Lincoln, and both Roosevelts, of course, chose the interpretations of legislators who had been elected by the people. But, Dworkin writes, Hand and the rest "wrongly rejected an apparently paradoxical possibility that was difficult to see in the years in which his opinions were formed but is more evident now." The more evident paradox, Dworkin continues, is that the "individual can in fact exercise the moral responsibilities of citizenship better when final decisions involving constitutional values are removed from ordinary politics and assigned to courts whose decisions are meant to turn on principle, not on the weight of numbers or the balance of political influence." Whose decisions are meant to turn on principle? On whose principles? Perhaps the principles of angels?

Dworkin believes the judicial process is better than the legislative process. The judicial branch deals with "matters of fundamental principle," and is concerned with reasoned moral argument. The legislative process is dominated by political pressure groups who bribe or blackmail legislators. "Ordinary politics" generally aim at political compromise rather than "reasoned argument elaborating underlying moral principles." The judicial process is also, Dworkin believes, more democratic than the legislative. Legislative decisions are "likely to be governed by what most people want" and consequently don't provoke much public debate. Judicial decisions, however, do not give the majority a role in the process and are likely to be contrary to the majority's wishes. They will consequently provoke more debate. Dworkin concludes the judicial process is more democratic than the political because it provokes more debate.

Dworkin's logic could be tighter. If judicial decisions were in fact apolitical (if that is possible) and based only on principle, public debate of the subject would be meaningless. The public does not debate issues for its amusement. Public debate is carried out for the purpose of gaining influence. The debate that Dworkin values occurs only because the people understand that judicial decisions are political and can be influenced. It may be that organized lobby groups have less influence in the courthouse than in the legislature, but the debate that Dworkin values is really intended to produce exactly the type of political result Dworkin decries. What we are left with is a small, unelected, second-chance legislature. That is not a principled process.

Justices in Hand's day, Dworkin writes, "treated constitutional issues as more conceptual than moral, and rarely brought moral argument explicitly into their opinions." But times have changed for the better; the process of nominating justices, he writes, is "more open" than it once was, and "allows the public to participate more effectively." Further, Dworkin writes: "Constitutional jurisprudence has improved since then, and Supreme Court opinions are more explicitly concerned with moral argument." And who does the reader think is good at bringing us messages about moral principles and issues? Yes, angels, all kinds, archangels, seraphim, and cherubim. Nine to sit on the Court to make a choir and little bands of lesser angels to hover around and write about them.

Jefferson's solution is the only democratic one—each new majority should write its own fundamental law. As he wrote to Samuel Kercheval in July of 1816:

> Let us [not] weakly believe that one generation is not as capable as another of taking care of itself, and of ordering its own affairs. Each generation is as independent of the preceding, as that was of all which had gone before. It

has, then, like them, a right to choose for itself the form of government it
believes most promotive of its own happiness.

Earlier, in 1789, he had written to Madison that he thought it self-
evident

that the earth belongs in *usufruct* [trust] to the living, that the dead have
neither powers nor rights over it . . . . No society can make a perpetual
constitution, or even a perpetual law. The earth belongs always to the living
generation; they may manage it then, and what proceeds from it, as they
please, during their usufruct. . . . Every constitution then, and every law,
naturally expires, at the end of thirty-four years. If it is enforced longer, it is
an act of force and not of right.

The difference between Marshall's original compact theory and
Jefferson's continuing consent theory is not academic.   In the
Dartmouth College case (1819), John Marshall used the Contract
Clause to deny the state legislature the power to amend a charter
granted by George III. Jefferson wrote to Governor Plumer on July
16, 1816 that our lawyers and priests generally teach that "*preceding
generations held the earth more freely then we do*; had a right to
impose laws on us, unalterable by ourselves, and that we, in like
manner, can make laws and impose burdens on future generations,
which they will have no right to alter, in fine, that the earth belongs
to the dead and not the living" (emphasis added). Judicial review,
Jefferson believed, gave the Supreme Court the power to vote the
dead.

Jefferson wrote to John Eppes in 1813, that we may consider each
generation "as a distinct nation, with a right, by the will of the
majority, to bind themselves, but none to bind the succeeding
generation, more than the inhabitants of another country." Or the
case may be likened, Jefferson said, "to the ordinary one of a tenant
for life, who may hypothecate the land for his debts, during the
continuance of his usufruct; but at his death, the reversioner (who is
also for life only) receives it exonerated from all burthen":

The earth belongs to the living, not to the dead. . . . The generations of men
may be considered as bodies or corporations.   Each generation has the
usufruct of the earth during the period of its continuance. When it ceases to
exist, the usufruct passes on to the succeeding generation, free and
unincumbered, and so on, successively, from one generation to another

forever. . . .[Is a new generation] bound to acknowledge the debt, to consider the preceding generation as having had a right to eat up the whole soil of their country, in the course of a life, to alienate it from them, (for it would be an alienation to the creditors,) and would they think themselves either legally or morally bound to give up their country and emigrate to another for subsistence.

Finally, in 1825, Jefferson summed up his idea as follows:

That our Creator made the earth for the use of the living and not of the dead; that those who exist not can have no use nor right in it: no authority or power over it; that one generation of men cannot foreclose or burden its use to another, which comes to it in its own right and by the same divine beneficence; that a preceding generation cannot bind a succeeding one by its laws or contracts, these deriving their obligation from the will of the existing majority, and that majority being removed by death, another comes in its place with a will equally free to make its own laws and contracts; These are axioms so self-evident that no explanation can make them plainer; for he is not to be reasoned with who says that non-existence can control existence, or that nothing can move something.

The current majority in the United States is miserable because of mental chains—it believes itself bound by a past that has burdened the present with a perpetual debt and a ruling judiciary. Jefferson would tell it to break the chains.

4

The Result—A Society Designed
by the Judiciary

San Francisco District Attorney Rothmo and
Judge Bannerman explaining to Inspector
Harry Callahan why they were releasing
Scorpio, who had kidnapped, raped, and
buried alive a fourteen-year-old girl, Mary-Ann
Deegan:

D.A.: *You're lucky I'm not indicting you for
assault with intent to commit murder.*

Harry Callahan: *What?*

D.A.: *Where the hell does it say you got a right
to kick down doors, torture suspects, deny medical attention and legal counsel? Where have you
been? Does Escobedo ring a bell? Miranda? I
mean you must have heard of the 4th
Amendment. What I'm saying is the man had
rights.*

H.C.: *Well I'm all broken up about that man's
rights.*

D.A.: *You should be. I've got news for you
Callahan. As soon as he's well enough to leave
the hospital, he walks.*

H.C.: *What are you talking about?*

D.A.: *He's free.*

113

> Judge Bannerman: *Well, in my opinion, the search of the suspect's quarters was illegal, evidence obtained thereby, such as that hunting rifle for instance, is inadmissible in court. You should have gotten a search warrant. I'm sorry but it's that simple.*
>
> H.C.: *Search warrant? There was a girl dying.*
>
> D.A.: *She was in fact dead according to the medical report.*
>
> H.C.: *But I didn't know that.*
>
> J.B.: *The court would have to recognize the police officer's legitimate concern for the girl's life but there is no way they can possibly condone police torture. All evidence concerning the girl, the suspect's confession, all physical evidence, would have to be excluded. The suspect's rights were violated under the 4th and 5th and probably the 6th and 14th Amendments.*
>
> H.C.: *And what about Mary-Ann Deegan's rights? I mean she's raped and left in a hole to die, who speaks for her?*
>
> D.A.: *The District Attorney's Office.*
>
> —*Dirty Harry* (1971) Warner Bros.

What happened when justices who were part of the adversarial culture got hold of the power to "twist and shape" the Constitution into a form that pleased them? About what you'd expect.

The Court took on the role of the protector of individual rights and self-expression against the will of the oppressive bourgeois majority. Crime, in this context, is a form of self-expression as well as social protest. The Court, in a series of decisions, created new rights for criminal defendants, atheists, prisoners, homosexuals, the mentally ill, illegal aliens, publishers of pornography, and others. In each case, the Court overturned the actions of the local police or board of education, or the state laws under which the local officials acted. The Court routinely denied the majority will. The federal judiciary, Thomas and Mary Edsall write in *Chain Reaction* (1991), "and the federal regulatory apparatus adopted remedies that sharply increased the political, economic, and social costs of the civil rights movement, including busing, affirmative action, strict legislative redistricting requirements, and a widening system of racial preferences."

The following major issues are those that largely determine the quality of life.

Criminal Law Enforcement. The FBI reports, for 1992, that one violent crime occurred every 22 seconds and that 83 percent of Americans will be victims of violent crime in their lifetime. For the past six years, in New York City, there has been one rape every three hours. Violent crime, as noted earlier, rose from 288,460 in 1960 to 387,390 in 1965 to 875,910 in 1973 to 1,932,270 in 1992. At the same time, the likelihood of punishment for a violent crime has dropped:

	Murder	Rape	Forcible Assault	Aggravated Robbery
1960	92%	73%	76%	39%
1965	92	64	73	38
1992	65	52	56	24

Meanwhile, the Court has pushed the cost of incarcerating a prisoner in New York to about $60,000 per convict per year—well beyond what the society can afford.

Public Schools. The per student cost of a child in the public school system, *The New York Times* reports, stated in constant 1990 dollars, rose from $1,500 in 1960 to $6,000 in 1990. The schools are nonetheless used less and less by the middle class who believe they are dangerous and inferior.

Affirmative Action. Encouraged by the Supreme Court, although inconsistent with equal opportunity and disliked by the majority of Americans.

Cultural Issues. The Court last year held that goat, sheep, cow, pig, dog, cat and turtle sacrifice was acceptable as freedom of religion. The courts have emptied the insane asylums onto city streets. New York, in 1955 had 93,000 patients in its mental hospitals; in 1992 they had 11,000. Where are the 82,000?

Voting Rights. The Court supervises racially defined districts to include just the right amount of racial balancing.

On these large issues, the Court has consistently overturned the plans of the majority. For the past thirty years, the Court has worked its major change by interpreting general words like freedom of speech, due process, and equal protection; words that can have any meaning the interpreter wants. The justices pour meaning into these words from their values that come from the adversarial culture and its inveterate hostility to bourgeois society. For example, in 1993 the Hialeah City Council adopted an ordinance barring animal sacrifices in the city. That seems reasonable, but when the city was sued by the Santeria Church, the angels did not bring heavenly tidings to the Hialeah Council. Instead, Justice Kennedy found in *Church of the Lukumi Babalu Aye, Inc. v. City of Hialeah,* (1993), that "the laws in question were enacted by officials who did not understand, failed to perceive, or chose to ignore the fact that their official actions violated the Nation's essential commitment to religious freedom." Not understanding, or failing to perceive, or choosing to ignore the constitution are terrible accusations. But possibly, just possibly, the Hialeah City Council, like almost everybody else in the country, didn't think that sacrificing goats, sheep, cows, pigs, dogs, cats, and turtles had anything to do with the Nation's essential commitment to religious freedom. Recently, the Hawaii Supreme Court ruled that refusing to license the marriage of gay couples, thus depriving them of financial and legal benefits, violated the Due Process Clause. The Supreme Court has affirmed an Eleventh Circuit Court of Appeals ruling that Cobb County, Georgia was violating the U.S. Constitution by having a bronze plaque of the Ten Commandments on its county courthouse wall. The federal court said that the county could either take down the plaque *or* it could place alongside it a plaque commemorating the Code of Hammurabi, a Babylonian ruler from the eighteenth century B.C.

John Stuart Mill said an individual can do anything as long as he does not harm another, but that is not such a clear standard; for example, what about crazy people, beggars, brothels and prostitutes in the street? It's true you don't have to pay or use them, but who wants to live in the middle of such a mess? Why can't a reasonable majority say we don't want to. Why does the majority have to be told that begging, in the stilted academic language of the courts, "implicates expressive conduct or communicative activity" for purposes of First Amendment analysis? And that begging, as the Second Circuit said in *Loper v. New York City Police Dept.*:

> frequently is accompanied by speech indicating the need for food, shelter, clothing, medical care or transportation. Even without particularized speech, however, the presence of an unkempt and disheveled person holding out his or her hand or a cup to receive a donation itself conveys a message of need for support and assistance. We see little difference between those who solicit for organized charities and those who solicit for themselves in regard to the message conveyed.

The Court considers the individual to be in an adversarial role to society and the state. Its rhetoric is favorable to the individual and hostile to the society, legislature, and the majority. Theodore H. White wrote in *The Making of the Presidency, 1968* that "[i]n this new climate the ancient balance between individual and state had been tipped farther than before: the individual was now the center point of concern, his expression of self the highest good; and the state was his enemy. In this climate, the courts now saw their highest duty not as the defense of state or of order, but defense of the individual *against* the state at extremes of judgment unprecedented in jurisprudence" (emphasis in original). This is natural enough since the Court believes its purpose is to protect the individual from the oppressive bourgeois majority. The Court does not recognize the moral sense of the community or the legitimate demands of society.

Liberal democracy, for the past fifty years, has been in urgent conflict with the two ugly sisters, nazism and communism. Professor Gertrude Himmelfarb in her new book, *On Looking into the Abyss*, asks how can a "society that is individualistic, pluralistic, pacific, devoted to private pleasures and domestic tranquility prevail against an enemy that is collectivist, authoritarian, militaristic, mobilized for power and conquest?" The answer, she continues, is that "totalitarianism is not only oppressive and murderous; it is inefficient and fatally vulnerable." As Eric Hoffer wrote in the *Ordeal of Change* (1963), the machine does not work smoothly if "you have to deafen ears with propaganda, crack the whip of Terror, and keep pushing people around."

Now, says Professor Himmelfarb, we must confront another problem, not how liberalism can defend itself against totalitarianism "but how it can defend itself against itself—against its own weaknesses and excesses." How can a society that celebrates the virtues of "liberty, individuality, variety and tolerance sustain itself when those virtues, carried to extreme, threaten to subvert that liberal society and with it those very virtues?" She traces the contradictions of classical liberalism to John Stuart Mill's *On Liberty*.

Mill writes, prematurely as it turned out, that the problem of liberty is no longer the problem of political liberty—the struggle of oppressed people against a tyrannical regime. Mill believed that problem had been solved by the establishment of popular government. Instead, he thought, the problem facing liberty was "social tyranny" exercised by the populace itself over the individual. "One very simple principle," he writes, should determine "the nature and limits of power which can be legitimately exercised by society over the individual." Mill said his principle was intended to limit not only the majority's right to impose legal penalties but also the "moral coercion of public opinion." Mill's principle is:

> that the sole end for which mankind are warranted, individually or collectively, in interfering with the liberty of action of any of their number, is self-protection. That the only purpose for which power can be rightfully exercised over any member of a civilized community, against his will, is to prevent harm to others. His own good, either physical or moral, is not a sufficient warrant.

Most readers will probably agree with Mill's "very simple principle." But there are problems with it, and these problems turn on who gets to decide what amounts to "self-protection" and "harm to others." When Mill identified this principle as the sole justification for interfering with individual freedom, he did not specify who gets to decide how it applies. The majority of a community may have one view of what "harm to others" amounts to, and a court may have another, particularly when the court is not inconvenienced by the results of its orders. The majority may see more harm in letting a guilty child murderer walk free because the police verbally persuaded a confession from him than they do in allowing police to question the accused without a lawyer present. The majority may feel that the same rules of probable cause that apply when police apprehend a suspected murderer should apply to motorists at sobriety checkpoints. The majority may not be offended by allowing a nativity scene on the courthouse lawn at Christmas, or a tablet with the Ten Commandments on the courthouse wall. The majority may not wish to spend $60,000 per inmate on prisons with a gymnasium, a law library, backgammon tournaments, and HBO. The majority may feel that "harm to others" occurs when race-based standards are applied to hiring, promotions, the awarding of public contracts, the sale of public assets, voting, and college admissions.

The Supreme Court consistently comes down against society—the majority—by requiring it to show a direct and perceptible harm from the individual's conduct. Peculiarly, and contradictorily, where the issue is whether the individual is harmed by the majority's action, for example, school prayer or Christmas crèche displays, the Court accepts the individual's subjective and psychological harm as real.

The Court permits government to be paternalistic on a host of physical and social matters, but has ruled others off limits, labelling them as constitutionally protected. Permissible physical paternalism includes legislation aimed at wages, work hours, working conditions, food safety, pollution, smoking, and drunk driving. A good deal of social paternalism not directly related to physical conditions is allowed. These measures include affirmative action, racial balancing, multicultural and sex education, abortion, and so on. Some forms of speech or conduct, however, are exempt even if they have physical consequences the community feels are undesirable. These include such things as pornography, obscene or blasphemous acts, and acts of "symbolic speech," like flag burning. At any given time, there seems to be an area of moral individualism to which the Court has decided to give absolute protection. The protection is usually afforded by putting an impossible burden on the state to justify its law, for example, requiring it to show that it has a "compelling interest" (whatever that is), or that it could not accomplish its purpose by some other means (which it always could), or that the interest of the community does not "weigh as heavily" or "balance" favorably against the wishes of the individual.

What is off limits and what is not is, under judicial review, determined by the Court's conception of a good society. Take the recent comments of retiring Justice Harry Blackmun on the death penalty. Though the death penalty is allowed by the Fifth Amendment, as long as it is administered with due process of law, Justice Blackmun declared that he disagreed. In an opinion handed down by the Court in February, 1994, Blackmun concluded that "the death penalty experiment has failed," and that capital punishment had proven to be a "delusion." Consequently, he said, "because I conclude that no sentence of death may be constitutionally imposed," there is no need to address the details of death sentence appeals: "From this day forward, I no longer shall tinker with the machinery of death."

Sometimes, judges are not as candid about imposing their subjective values as Justice Blackmun. Justice Ginsburg, at her confirmation hearing, said one of her "most sacred duties" would be "not to read her convictions into the Constitution." Justice Breyer, at his confirmation hearing, said that his "subjective preferences" did not play any part in his judicial process. In a recent ruling that the "Equal Protection" clause of the Fourteenth Amendment required the admission of a female applicant to the Citadel, a formerly all-male military college in South Carolina, the district court judge declared: "It is not an occasion where one judge votes his will. In this matter, the Constitution of the United States alone speaks and determines the outcome of this controversy." How does it speak to him?

Judicial intervention shapes the society in ways that legislative majorities never would. A legislator, because he desires to be reelected, will not take up controversial subjects which will aggravate a significant amount of his voters. What majority, for example, would require a state to give welfare to nonresidents (*Shapiro*); or require a state to provide free hospital care to indigent nonresidents (*Maricopa*); or require a policeman to warn a captive caught running out of a bank with a bag of money that he should not tell the police the truth about what he is doing (*Miranda*); or find prison officials liable to a prison inmate for harm inflicted by other inmates (*Brennan*); or find a prison inmates's exposure to second-hand tobacco smoke could constitute cruel and unusual punishment (*Helling*); or allow police to set up road blocks to stop citizens without probable cause in the hope they may be drunk, not carrying their car registration, or not wearing their seatbelts (*Michigan State Police*). The legislator's motivation may not be noble or brave but the result is what Jefferson wanted—a government that is not "energetic."

America, until the 1960s, was a liberal country in the traditional, nonabsolutist sense.   Jefferson, of course, was against any governmental control of thought or ideas. The people's political wisdom and virtue, as he wrote in *Notes on Virginia*, will be expressed if there is a free debate of ideas: "It is error alone which needs the support of government. Truth can stand by itself. Subject opinion to coercion: whom will you make your inquisitors? Fallible men, men governed by bad passions, by private as well as public reasons. And why subject it to coercion?"

Since the 1960s, led by the Court, we have experimented with judicially enforced absolute individual liberty. The Court's principle, however, cannot be theoretically, or plausibly, limited— a society run on the absolute individual liberty principle cannot prevent anything, not panhandling, not prostitution (no direct and perceptible harm to others), not drugs, and, indeed, not murder.   Why should the murderer's absolute right to self-expression be outweighed by the victim's right to live? The Court is giving us a society in which there are no majority rules at all. But who wants to live in that kind of society?

Professor Robert Nagel writes in *Public Interest* (Summer, 1994) that the culture wars over homosexuality have locked American society in a "ferocious struggle over defining the morality of sexual behavior, the meaning of psychological health, and the function of family life." While the rhetoric on both sides is often extravagant, it reflects real and irreconcilable differences on matters that are crucial to individuals, families, and society.   Jefferson believed that democracy was the best way to deal with difficult problems; as he wrote to Lafayette, "the good sense of our people will direct the boat ultimately to its proper point." But, increasingly, Nagel writes, "it appears that the nation's judges will attempt to extricate us from our dilemma. A gathering consensus in respectable circles holds not only that courts should resolve the important disputes about public policy on homosexuality, but that they can do so in a way that does not require anyone to answer the underlying moral questions." Midshipman Joseph Steffan was dismissed from the Naval Academy in 1987 after he stated he was a homosexual, which was a violation of Defense Department regulations. Chief Judge Abner J. Mikva of the District of Columbia Circuit Court of Appeals conceded the military could prohibit homosexual conduct, but found that it is "inherently unreasonable" to presume that a person is more likely to break a rule simply because of intention or desire. The military's finding that the presence of homosexuals harms morale and discipline was set aside by the court because it "depends solely upon the prejudice of third parties." The court's opinion, later vacated, also rejected the military's argument that the presence of homosexuals invades the privacy of heterosexual servicemen: "The argument that homosexuals will stare is very similar to the argument that they will engage in homosexual acts . . . . The argument that heterosexuals will fear such staring is, in turn, a version of the argument that government should be allowed to give effect to the irrational fears and stereotypes of third parties." Professor Nagel concludes the court's analysis is "a smoke screen necessary because the crucial propositions that underlie the decision are doubtful and far beyond the competence of any court."

Professor James Davison Hunter reports on abortion, another major front in the culture wars, in his book, *Before the Shooting Begins* (1994). The exercise of state power, Hunter writes, "can never provide any democratically sustainable solution to the culture war." The only sustainable resolution is some working agreement on the common good. The polarized rhetoric of the abortion debate is misleading, Hunter says, because the majority of Americans have very complex and ambivalent beliefs on the subject. 80 percent of Americans say abortion is acceptable if the womans life is endangered; 70 percent if the pregnancy is the result of rape; but less than 10 percent if abortion is used as a repeated method of birth control.

Hunter concludes that the "rhetoric of the public debate is more polarized than we are as a people." He believes this may be true on a number of other issues as well, including race, the arts, education, family and family values, and sexuality. The problem, he believes, is that the democracy is not functioning; certainly, he adds, "the judiciary has not helped matters." Litigation presents stark alternatives and wrongly focuses the public debate. The demoralized democracy consistently is presented false choices, for example, whether we favor women or unborn babies. If the democracy can be renewed, he concludes, we may discover that the rhetoric of the current debate is artificially polarized. But, to find out, we first have to restore the democracy.

We have always known, Himmelfarb writes, that absolute power tends to corrupt absolutely, and we are now discovering that absolute liberty also tends to corrupt absolutely. The "tendency of absolute liberty," Himmelfarb writes, is "to subvert the very liberty it seeks to preserve." Absolute liberty acts that way because it invalidates "all those other principles—history, custom, law, interest, opinion, religion—which have traditionally served to support particular liberties." The "absolutistic doctrine may have the unwitting effect of depriving the most essential liberties of the security they enjoy under more traditional, modest auspices." The judicial enforcement of absolute liberty undercuts the nonjudicial supports for freedom, including tradition, culture and, of course, the other two branches. The Court, for example, has replaced the traditional nonjudicial supports for free speech with its own complicated formulae. The First Amendment's clear and direct language prohibiting Congress from "abridging the freedom of speech is reformulated by the Court in *United States v. O'Brien* (1968) (upholding conviction of O'Brien for burning his Selective Service registration certificate before a sizable crowd) to read:

> This Court has held that when "speech" and "nonspeech" elements are combined in the same course of conduct, a sufficiently important governmental interest in regulating the nonspeech element can justify incidental limitations on First Amendment freedoms. To characterize the quality of the governmental interest which must appear, the Court has

employed a variety of descriptive terms: compelling; substantial; subordinating; paramount; cogent; strong. Whatever imprecision inheres in these terms, we think it clear that a government regulation is sufficiently justified if it is within the constitutional power of the Government; if it furthers an important or substantial governmental interest; if the governmental interest is unrelated to the suppression of free expression; and if the incidental restriction on alleged First Amendment freedoms is no greater than is essential to the furtherance of that interest.

Would the people ever have adopted that Amendment? The Court's formulae lead to bizarre and unexplainable results—protection for the burning of flags but not for the burning of draft registration cards—protection for yard signs, obscenity, and nude dancing, but not for Frank Snepp's book critical of the precipitous U.S. withdrawal from the Saigon Embassy roof—leaving behind the records of many who had assisted the U.S. If those decisions can be reconciled, as Jefferson wrote to William Johnson in 1823, "I surrender human reason as a vain and useless faculty, given to bewilder, and not to guide us." The Court's program, as Robert Nagel writes, "has done great damage to the public understanding and appreciation of the principle of free speech by making it seem trivial, foreign, and unnecessarily costly."

And when the "absolute principle proves inadequate to the exigencies of social life," Himmelfarb writes, "it is abandoned absolutely," replaced not by a more moderate form of liberty but by immoderate government control. The principle of absolute liberty makes distinctions of degree unimportant. "Any liberty that falls short of" the absolute "is seen as fatally flawed." A traditional nonabsolutist liberal society is "deemed to be as illiberal and illegitimate as a despotic society." Any compromise is treason. This is the logic of the "postmodernist critique of all societies, including the most liberal, as equally 'tyrannical,' 'authoritarian,' 'hegemonic,' or 'totalizing.'"

There are no constitutionally absolute rights because there are ethically no absolute rights. As C.E. Merriam, wrote in *A History of American Political Theories* (1903), values conflict with one another—we want security but we also want adventure—we want to be just but find we cannot be just without being cruel—we want to be loyal but find that truth may conflict with loyalty.

Those who have experienced the tyranny of totalitarianism can appreciate how very different that is from the "social tyranny" of liberal democracy. They also appreciate the dangers of an absolute principle of liberty that gives little support for those private and public virtues required of a liberal democracy. Vaclav Havel writes:

> The return of freedom to a place that became morally unhinged has produced something that it clearly had to produce, and therefore something we might have expected. But it has turned out to be far more serious than anyone could have predicted: an enormous and blindingly visible explosion of every imaginable human vice. A wide range of questionable or at least ambivalent human tendencies, quietly encouraged over the years and, at the same time, quietly pressed to serve the daily operation of the totalitarian system, has suddenly been liberated, as it were, from its straitjacket and given free rein at last. The authoritarian regime imposed a certain order—if that is the right expression for it—on these vices (and in doing so "legitimized" them, in a sense). This order has now been broken down, but a new order that would limit rather than exploit these vices, an order based on a free accepted responsibility to and for the whole of society, has not yet been built, nor could it have been, for such an order takes years to develop and cultivate. And thus we are witnesses to a bizarre state of affairs: society has freed itself, true, but in some ways it behaves worse than when it was in chains.

Havel's society, which freed itself from a totalitarian system, will act badly for a time—just to test out its new found freedoms. But the people will find anarchy to be unpleasant and uncomfortable and will develop a new order based on freely accepted responsibility to and for the whole of society. The American version of a "blindingly visible explosion of every imaginable vice" does not come from a healthy revolution, but from the judicial overthrow of a traditional nonabsolutist liberal democracy. The society created by the judiciary has unexpected characteristics—first of all, it is unable to deal with the lawless. Western society has known for a long time how to deal with amoral, bloodthirsty people who set upon citizens, but the judicial society cannot. At the same time, it presses down very hard on the law-abiding citizen. Government is more and more intrusive into the everyday life of the majority. The courts, and the police, find the law-abiding easier to push around than the lawless. The miscreant common man is hounded for everything from seatbelt violations to burning leaves on a crisp October night.

The result of freedom for the lawless and oppression for the law-abiding is called "anarcho-tyranny" by *Washington Times* columnist Sam Francis. The "anarcho" part of "anarcho-tyranny" is that the judiciary has made it so difficult and expensive to deal with the violent criminal that society must tolerate a form of anarchy at his hands. The "tyranny" part is that the country's law enforcement machinery, unable to do anything about violent crime, has expanded the definition of crime to include ordinary activities of the law-abiding. For awhile, under Jimmy Carter, it was a crime to turn up the thermostat.

The American "explosion of every imaginable vice" is described by Senator Daniel Patrick Moynihan in a recent *American Scholar* (Winter, 1993) essay titled "Defining Deviancy Down." He includes as deviancy: criminality, family breakdown—almost 30 percent of American children are born to unmarried women—and mental illness—thousands of ill people have been released onto city streets to sleep in doorways and freeze on grates. They are, the Senator writes, part of the landscape. Moynihan argues that the epidemic of deviancy has reached such incomprehensible proportions that we have adopted a singular form of denial—we lower the threshold of what we call normal till the volume of redefined deviancy is within manageable proportions. We redefine deviancy down to relabel as normal what, when we were a healthy society, we called deviant.

Charles Krauthammer describes a complementary social phenomenon in his *New Republic* (November 22, 1993) article titled "Defining Deviancy Up." At the same time we are, as Moynihan correctly points out, redefining the deviant as normal, we are also redefining the normal as deviant. The "seedbed of deviancy," we have finally figured out, is the "Ozzie and Harriet family, rife with abuse and molestation." Deviant thinking and speech has become a major issue. Many of us "are guilty of disordered thinking for harboring—beneath the bland niceties of middle-class life—racist, misogynist, homophobic and other corrupt and corrupting insensitiv-ities." Campus speech codes require reeducation if a student expresses incorrect ideas. What is the purpose of defining deviancy up? Krauthammer finds two good reasons. The first is distraction. Since we are helpless "in the face of the explosion of real criminality," we satisfy society's need to police its norms by crusading against bad ideas and behavior. The police get a big bonus—a better class of offender—"the guilt-ridden bourgeois, the vulnerable college student, is a far easier object of social control than the hardened criminal or the raving lunatic."

The second reason is that defining deviancy up is a new stick for the adversarial culture to beat the common American with. During the cold war, the estranged intellectual elite expressed its hostility to America by the theory of moral equivalence—Western culture, we were told, was the moral equivalent of the Soviet. Liberal capitalism, moral equivalence theory went, was at least as cruel, dangerous, and oppressive as Soviet-style socialism. That theory, however, could not be maintained after the oppressed people threw that empire over. But it now returns in a domestic version: "The deviant is declared normal. And the normal is unmasked as deviant. That, of course, makes us all that much more morally equal." The moral superiority to which bourgeois normalcy pretends vanishes with the moral convergence of the normal and the deviant.

Jefferson and Madison believed, of course, in free will and individual liberty but also in the common good—what they called "republican virtue." Madison said: "I go on this great republican principle, that the people will have virtue and intelligence to select men of virtue and wisdom. . . . To suppose that any form of government will secure liberty or happiness without any virtue in the people, is a chimerical idea."

Democracy, as Jefferson said, is more than a political system, it is a way of life, an attitude toward people. "Why," asks Sidney Hook, "should we treat individuals of unequal talents and endowments as persons who are equally entitled to relevant consideration and care?" The answer to that is the next, and last, stop.

Conclusion

The American Revolution is not finished yet. Near the heart of America is the unresolved conflict between our two most basic principles: one, that all power derives from the people, and two, that certain inalienable rights are immune from government power. This conflict, in some way, has to be resolved and the critical issue is *who will decide* if government has gone beyond its proper powers and is disturbing inalienable rights. That issue, in turn, depends on whether the Jeffersonian view of the nature of man or the Hamiltonian prevails. Jefferson wrote to Madison in 1787: "After all, it is my principle that the will of the majority should always prevail." Hamilton, on the other hand, wrote of the "amazing violence and turbulence of the democratic spirit." Other values cluster around each man's basic premise. Jefferson's belief in the common man led him to believe in weak government, unenergetic legislatures, low taxes, no debt, and government as close to the people as possible. The critical point was self rule. Hamilton's lack of faith in the common man led him to believe in a strong national government, a social and economic aristocracy, an industrial state, taxes, debt, and, of course, judicial review.

The two views have been at war from the beginning when both men were in Washington's cabinet. The country prospered as long as neither view could gain a complete victory, as long as there was a tension between the democratic impulse and the force of national unity. Each view corrected the bias of the other. Marshall's nationalistic decisions, the Civil War, the Civil War Amendments, industrialization, and the creation of a national market were successes for Hamilton. Jefferson's insistence on the right of the current majority to shape its own institutions prevented Hamilton's

129

principles from developing a privileged aristocracy. Jefferson's belief in self-rule was maintained by Lincoln, who said a constitutional majority "is the only true sovereign of a free people." Theodore Roosevelt, around the turn of the century, reaffirmed the vitality of Jefferson's belief in majority rule in the post-Civil War world. Franklin Roosevelt, on behalf of the majority, checked the Court in the 1930s. The majority remained in control until around 1965, when the events outlined in this book started to take place. Since 1965, with Hamilton's principles in complete sway, the country has done badly.

The earth belongs to the living, Jefferson said, and each generation should shape its own law and constitution. All issues, in a constitutional convention, are on the table: "No restriction," Livingston told the 1821 New York Convention, "limits our proceedings. We are standing on the foundations of society." One thing the people might want to do, while they are looking at the foundations of society, is to limit the power of the judiciary. Perhaps, as Jefferson suggested, by appointment of justices for six years, with reappointment by the president and approval of both Houses. Or perhaps by adopting Theodore Roosevelt's proposal to give the people a chance to overrule the Court after the Court overrules the people. Either way, as Jefferson wrote on April 20, 1806, would finally correct "the error in our Constitution which makes any branch independent of the nation." It could give us, Jefferson wrote, "a renewed extension of the term of our lease."

Governments are republican, Jefferson wrote, "in proportion as they embody the will of the people and execute it." The last time, according to consistent polling, that Americans felt good about themselves and their government was during the presidency of John Kennedy. The system, at the time, was majoritarian. Since then, majority rule has determined less and less and judicial rule has determined more and more. Major areas of the citizen's life, his education, his job, and his vote, are controlled by the courts, not the legislature. Jefferson said elections were "remedies" but they are not remedies against an independent judiciary. The state and national legislatures are blocked by the courts out of the critical areas that determine the quality of the citizen's life. Increasingly unused to power, the legislatures exercise awkwardly the power they do have.

The people believe their representatives have failed. During the 1992 election, *The Economist* wrote: "The democratic bond between the people and their elected representatives appears to have snapped."

Minority rule, by the Court, or other guardians, is obviously no system for a free people. The danger of minority rule is that there is no way of stopping it when it goes wrong. The people cannot make it accountable. The minority devoutly believes in itself and, rather than change direction, will lead the country over the cliff. The Court, as Jefferson said, is "the germ of dissolution of our federal government." Angels who fly too near the sun may burn their wings and fall to earth.

A country run by the majority is not a perfect society, but it is able to educate a child, and a citizen can walk down the street without getting hit on the head. For the rest, as Jefferson said, the society will be as good as the people. How hard is it to limit the unlimited Court? Not very. Jefferson said that chains are always self-imposed. No past decision irrevocably binds the present or future. He hoped the Declaration of Independence was the signal to the world, to some parts sooner, to some parts later, but finally to all, to arouse "men to burst the chains under which monkish ignorance and superstition had persuaded them to bind themselves, and to assume the blessings and security of self-government." The people were held down by the superstitions they believed—that kings ruled by divine prerogative—that man isn't capable of self-rule—that, in the case of a revolution, "it was the people who encroached on the sovereign, not the sovereign who usurped on the rights of the people."

A country run by guardians has a different character than one which is self-governing. Learned Hand wrote:

> For myself it would be most irksome to be ruled by a bevy of Platonic Guardians, even if I knew how to choose them, which I assuredly do not. If they were in charge, I should miss the stimulus of living in a society where I have, at least theoretically, some part in the direction of public affairs. Of course, I know how illusory would be the belief that my vote determined anything; but nevertheless when I go to the polls I have a satisfaction in the sense that we are all engaged in a common venture.

Hand recognized that modern government is large and remote, and not many issues are expressly fought out in elections. But we are still engaged in a common venture. The majority will make mistakes, but it will learn from its mistakes. Neither Jefferson nor Hand could figure out an effective alternative to majority rule. Hand, in 1932, advised against replacing democracy with guardians:

> And so when I hear so much impatient and irritable complaint, so much readiness to replace what we have by guardians for us all, those supermen, evoked somewhere from the clouds, whom none have seen and none are ready to name, I lapse into a dream, as it were. I see children playing on the grass; their voices are shrill and discordant as children's are; they are restive and quarrelsome; they cannot agree to any common plan; their play annoys them; it goes so poorly. *And one says, let us make Jack the master; Jack knows all about it; Jack will tell us what each is to do* and we shall all agree. But Jack is like all the rest; Helen is discontented with her part and Henry with his, and soon they fall again into their old state. No, *the children must learn to play by themselves; there is no Jack the master. And in the end slowly and with infinite disappointment they do learn a little; they learn to forbear, to reckon with one another, accept a little where they wanted much, to live and let live; to yield when they must yield*; perhaps, we may hope, not to take all they can. But the condition is that they shall be willing at least to listen to one another, to get the habit of pooling their wishes. *Somehow or other they must do this, if the play is to go on; maybe it will not, but there is no Jack*, in or out of the box, who can come to straighten the game. (Emphasis added)

There is no Jack the master. And there are no angels sent here to govern us.

Selected Reading List

Bancroft, George. *History of the United States: From the Discovery of the American Continent.* Boston: Charles C. Little and James Brown, 1845.

Black, Charles L. *The People and the Court: Judicial Review in a Democracy.* Westport, CT: Greenwood Press, 1977.

Blackstone, William. *Commentaries on the Laws of England.* Chicago: University of Chicago Press, 1979.

Bork, Robert H. *The Tempting of America: The Political Seduction of the Law.* New York: Free Press, 1990.

Boyd, Julian B., et al., eds. *The Papers of Thomas Jefferson.* 19 Vols. to date. Princeton, NJ: Princeton University Press, 1950--.

Calhoun, John C. *A Disquisition on Government and A Discourse on the Constitution and Government of the United States.* Columbia, S.C.: Printed by A.S. Johnston, 1851.

Commager, Henry Steele. *Majority Rule and Minority Rights,* New York: Oxford University Press, 1943.

Jefferson, Nationalism, and the Enlightenment. New York: George Braziller 1975.

Corwin, Edward S. *The Doctrine of Judicial Review.* Princeton, N.J.: Princeton University Press, 1914.

The Constitution and What it Means Today. Princeton, N.J.: Princeton University Press, 1920, 1946.

The Twilight of the Supreme Court: A History of Our Constitutional Theory, Hamdon, CT: Archon Books, 1970.

133

Court over Constitution: A Study of Judicial Review as an Instrument of Popular Government. Gloucester, Mass.: P.Smith, 1938.

Constitutional Revolution, Ltd. Claremont, CA: Claremont College, 1941.

Total War and the Constitution. New York: Alfred A. Knopf, 1947.

Cox, Archibald. *The Role of the Supreme Court in American Government.* New York: Oxford University Press, 1976.

Croly, Herbert D. *Progressive Democracy.* New York: Macmillan, 1914.

Douglas, William O. *We the Judges: Studies in American and Indian Constitutional Law from Marshall to Mukherja.* Garden City, NY: Doubleday and Company, Inc., 1956.

Dworkin, Ronald M. *Life's Dominion: An Argument About Abortion, Euthanasia, and Individual Freedom.* New York: Alfred A. Knopf, 1993.

Edsall, Thomas Byrne. *Chain Reaction: The Impact of Race, Rights, and Taxes on American Politics.* New York: W.W. Norton & Company, 1991.

Elkins, Stanley M. and McKitrick, Eric. *The Age of Federalism.* New York: Oxford University Press, 1993.

Fleming, Thomas. *The Politics of Human Nature.* New Brunswick, N.J.: Transaction Books, 1988.

Gunther, Gerald. *Learned Hand: The Man and the Judge.* New York: Alfred A. Knopf, 1994.

Hamilton, Alexander. *The Works of Alexander Hamilton.* (Henry Cabot Lodge, ed.) 12 Vols. New York: G.P. Putnam's Sons, 1903.

Hamilton, Alexander, James Madison, and John Jay. *The Federalist.* Rutland, VT.: Charles E. Tuttle Co., Inc., 1992.

Hand, Learned. *The Bill of Rights.* Cambridge, Mass.: Harvard University Press, 1958.

Himmelfarb, Gertrude. *On Looking into the Abyss: Untimely Thoughts on Culture and Society.* New York: Alfred A. Knopf, 1994.

Hoffer, Eric. *The Ordeal of Change.* New York: Harper & Row, 1967.

Hollander, Paul. *Anti-Americanism: Critiques at Home and Abroad, 1965-1990*. New York: Oxford University Press, 1992.

Hook, Sidney. *Education for Modern Man: A New Perspective*. New York: Humanities Press, 1973.

   Paradoxes of Freedom. Berkeley, CA: University of California Press, 1962.

Horowitz, Irving Louis. *Winners and Losers: Social and Political Polarities: America*. Durham, N.C. Duke University Press, 1984.

Hunter, James Davison. *Before the Shooting Begins: Searching for Democracy in America's Culture War*. New York: Free Press, 1994.

Jefferson, Thomas. *Notes on the State of Virginia*. New York: Harper & Row, 1964.

   The Complete Anas of Thomas Jefferson. (Franklin B. Sawvel, ed.) New York: Round Table Press, 1903.

   The Writings of Thomas Jefferson. (Ford, Paul Leicester. ed.) 10 vols. New York: G.P. Putnam's Sons, 1892-1899.

Koch, Adrienne. *Jefferson and Madison: The Great Collaboration*. New York: Alfred A. Knopf, 1950.

Locke, John. *Of Civil Government*. New York: E.P. Dutton, 1924.

Machiavelli, Niccolo. *The Discourses*. Harmondsworth, UK: Penguin Books, 1970.

Madison, James. *Papers*. (William T. Hutchison, et al., eds.) 17 vols. Chicago: University of Chicago Press and University of Virginia Press, 1962 ---.

Malone, Dumas. *Jefferson the President: First Term, 1801-1805*. Boston: Little, Brown and Company, 1970.

   Jefferson the President: Second Term, 1805-1809. Boston: Little, Brown and Company, 1974.

McDonald, Forrest. *The Presidency of Thomas Jefferson*. Lawrence, KS: University Press of Kansas, 1976.

Merriam, Charles Edward. *A History of American Political Theories*. New York: A.M. Kelley, 1969.

Mill, John Stuart. *On Liberty*. New York: W.W. Norton & Company, 1975.

Nagel, Robert F. *Constitutional Cultures: The Mentality and Consequences of Judicial Review*. Berkeley, CA: University of California Press, 1989.

Presser, Stephen D. *The Original Misunderstanding: The English, the Americans, and the Dialectic of Federalist Jurisprudence*. Durham, NC: Carolina Academic Press, 1991.

Ransom, William L. *Majority Rule and The Judiciary*. New York, Charles Scribner's Sons, 1912.

Roosevelt, Theodore. *Autobiography*. New York: Charles Scribner's Sons, 1913.

Solzhenitsyn, Aleksandr Isaevich. *Rebuilding Russia: Reflections and Tentative Proposals*. New York: Farrar, Straus and Giroux, 1991.

Taylor, John. *An Inquiry into the Principles and Policies of the Government of the United States*. Fredericksburg, VA: Green and Cady, 1814.

Thayer, James Bradley. *John Marshall*. New York: Da Capo Press, 1974.

Tocqueville, Alexis de. *Democracy in America*. Chicago: Encyclopedia Britannica, Inc., 1990.

White, Theodore H. *The Making of the President, 1960*. New York: Atheneum Publishers, 1961.

The Making of the President, 1968. New York: Atheneum, 1969.

Will, George, F. *Restoration: Congress, Term Limits, and the Recovery of Deliberative Democracy*. New York: Free Press. 1992.

Wilson, Clyde. ed. *The Essential Calhoun*. New Brunswick, NJ: Transaction Publishers, 1992.

Wright, Benjamin Fletcher. *Consensus and Continuity, 1776-1787*. New York: W.W. Norton & Company, 1967.

Index